C-2975   CAREER EXAMINATION SERIES

This is your
PASSBOOK for...

Inspector (Housing)

Test Preparation Study Guide
Questions & Answers

COPYRIGHT NOTICE

This book is SOLELY intended for, is sold ONLY to, and its use is RESTRICTED to individual, bona fide applicants or candidates who qualify by virtue of having seriously filed applications for appropriate license, certificate, professional and/or promotional advancement, higher school matriculation, scholarship, or other legitimate requirements of education and/or governmental authorities.

This book is NOT intended for use, class instruction, tutoring, training, duplication, copying, reprinting, excerption, or adaptation, etc., by:

1) Other publishers
2) Proprietors and/or Instructors of "Coaching" and/or Preparatory Courses
3) Personnel and/or Training Divisions of commercial, industrial, and governmental organizations
4) Schools, colleges, or universities and/or their departments and staffs, including teachers and other personnel
5) Testing Agencies or Bureaus
6) Study groups which seek by the purchase of a single volume to copy and/or duplicate and/or adapt this material for use by the group as a whole without having purchased individual volumes for each of the members of the group
7) Et al.

Such persons would be in violation of appropriate Federal and State statutes.

PROVISION OF LICENSING AGREEMENTS – Recognized educational, commercial, industrial, and governmental institutions and organizations, and others legitimately engaged in educational pursuits, including training, testing, and measurement activities, may address request for a licensing agreement to the copyright owners, who will determine whether, and under what conditions, including fees and charges, the materials in this book may be used them. In other words, a licensing facility exists for the legitimate use of the material in this book on other than an individual basis. However, it is asseverated and affirmed here that the material in this book CANNOT be used without the receipt of the express permission of such a licensing agreement from the Publishers. Inquiries re licensing should be addressed to the company, attention rights and permissions department.

All rights reserved, including the right of reproduction in whole or in part, in any form or by any means, electronic or mechanical, including photocopying, recording, or by any information storage and retrieval system, without permission in writing from the Publisher.

Copyright © 2024 by
National Learning Corporation

212 Michael Drive, Syosset, NY 11791
(516) 921-8888 • www.passbooks.com
E-mail: info@passbooks.com

PASSBOOK® SERIES

THE *PASSBOOK® SERIES* has been created to prepare applicants and candidates for the ultimate academic battlefield – the examination room.

At some time in our lives, each and every one of us may be required to take an examination – for validation, matriculation, admission, qualification, registration, certification, or licensure.

Based on the assumption that every applicant or candidate has met the basic formal educational standards, has taken the required number of courses, and read the necessary texts, the *PASSBOOK® SERIES* furnishes the one special preparation which may assure passing with confidence, instead of failing with insecurity. Examination questions – together with answers – are furnished as the basic vehicle for study so that the mysteries of the examination and its compounding difficulties may be eliminated or diminished by a sure method.

This book is meant to help you pass your examination provided that you qualify and are serious in your objective.

The entire field is reviewed through the huge store of content information which is succinctly presented through a provocative and challenging approach – the question-and-answer method.

A climate of success is established by furnishing the correct answers at the end of each test.

You soon learn to recognize types of questions, forms of questions, and patterns of questioning. You may even begin to anticipate expected outcomes.

You perceive that many questions are repeated or adapted so that you can gain acute insights, which may enable you to score many sure points.

You learn how to confront new questions, or types of questions, and to attack them confidently and work out the correct answers.

You note objectives and emphases, and recognize pitfalls and dangers, so that you may make positive educational adjustments.

Moreover, you are kept fully informed in relation to new concepts, methods, practices, and directions in the field.

You discover that you are actually taking the examination all the time: you are preparing for the examination by "taking" an examination, not by reading extraneous and/or supererogatory textbooks.

In short, this PASSBOOK®, used directedly, should be an important factor in helping you to pass your test.

INSPECTOR (HOUSING)

DUTIES

Inspectors (Housing), under general supervision, perform technical work in the inspection of dwellings and other structures for the enforcement of the Multiple Dwelling Law, Housing Maintenance Code and other laws, rules and regulations that govern occupancy, safety and sanitary conditions of such dwellings and structures. They make inspections of dwellings to insure compliance with the Multiple Dwelling Law, Housing Maintenance Code and other statutes; explain and interpret housing codes to property owners and tenants; inspect for illegal conversion of one or two family homes to multiple dwellings, or for change in occupancy or use of multiple dwellings; inspect rooms which are used for living quarters to determine whether they are crowded beyond ordinance requirements; check for adequacy of light and ventilation and plumbing facilities; check gas appliances in dwelling units for detection and measurement of emitted carbon monoxide; inspect yards, courts and occupied premises for the presence of garbage, refuse, stagnant water, sewage, improper drainage and other hazards or nuisances which might be present; perform inspections on any structure, part thereof or related areas based on citizens' complaints concerning lack of water, water leaks, piping noises, water hammer, etc.; insufficient or lack of heat when the outside temperature falls below specified amounts; unsanitary conditions in the public parts of buildings, yards, courts, areaways, alleyways, roofs, etc.; rodents and insect infestation and conducive conditions, and various damages such as holes in walls, floors, ceilings, broken locks on hallway doors, etc.; inspect heating and hot water plants, chimneys and flues for escape of gases, and for violations; investigate complaints and make emergency inspections of hazardous conditions created by explosions, fires; etc.; prepare reports of inspections and draw floor diagram for the official records of the Department; place violations on dwellings and prepare cases for court prosecution, appearing in court as witness; make such re-inspections as ordered by the court; may supervise Apprentice Inspectors (Housing); and operate a motor vehicle. All Inspectors (Housing) perform related work.

SCOPE OF THE EXAMINATION

The multiple-choice test may include questions on building mechanical systems such as plumbing, heating, ventilation and other parts of multiple dwellings such as windows, doors and public access areas; various building materials used in the construction of multiple dwellings; related trade practices such as carpentry, plumbing and plastering; comprehension and interpretation of housing laws, rules and regulations; filling out forms and preparing reports; and other related areas.

HOW TO TAKE A TEST

I. YOU MUST PASS AN EXAMINATION

A. *WHAT EVERY CANDIDATE SHOULD KNOW*

Examination applicants often ask us for help in preparing for the written test. What can I study in advance? What kinds of questions will be asked? How will the test be given? How will the papers be graded?

As an applicant for a civil service examination, you may be wondering about some of these things. Our purpose here is to suggest effective methods of advance study and to describe civil service examinations.

Your chances for success on this examination can be increased if you know how to prepare. Those "pre-examination jitters" can be reduced if you know what to expect. You can even experience an adventure in good citizenship if you know why civil service exams are given.

B. *WHY ARE CIVIL SERVICE EXAMINATIONS GIVEN?*

Civil service examinations are important to you in two ways. As a citizen, you want public jobs filled by employees who know how to do their work. As a job seeker, you want a fair chance to compete for that job on an equal footing with other candidates. The best-known means of accomplishing this two-fold goal is the competitive examination.

Exams are widely publicized throughout the nation. They may be administered for jobs in federal, state, city, municipal, town or village governments or agencies.

Any citizen may apply, with some limitations, such as the age or residence of applicants. Your experience and education may be reviewed to see whether you meet the requirements for the particular examination. When these requirements exist, they are reasonable and applied consistently to all applicants. Thus, a competitive examination may cause you some uneasiness now, but it is your privilege and safeguard.

C. *HOW ARE CIVIL SERVICE EXAMS DEVELOPED?*

Examinations are carefully written by trained technicians who are specialists in the field known as "psychological measurement," in consultation with recognized authorities in the field of work that the test will cover. These experts recommend the subject matter areas or skills to be tested; only those knowledges or skills important to your success on the job are included. The most reliable books and source materials available are used as references. Together, the experts and technicians judge the difficulty level of the questions.

Test technicians know how to phrase questions so that the problem is clearly stated. Their ethics do not permit "trick" or "catch" questions. Questions may have been tried out on sample groups, or subjected to statistical analysis, to determine their usefulness.

Written tests are often used in combination with performance tests, ratings of training and experience, and oral interviews. All of these measures combine to form the best-known means of finding the right person for the right job.

II. HOW TO PASS THE WRITTEN TEST

A. NATURE OF THE EXAMINATION

To prepare intelligently for civil service examinations, you should know how they differ from school examinations you have taken. In school you were assigned certain definite pages to read or subjects to cover. The examination questions were quite detailed and usually emphasized memory. Civil service exams, on the other hand, try to discover your present ability to perform the duties of a position, plus your potentiality to learn these duties. In other words, a civil service exam attempts to predict how successful you will be. Questions cover such a broad area that they cannot be as minute and detailed as school exam questions.

In the public service similar kinds of work, or positions, are grouped together in one "class." This process is known as *position-classification*. All the positions in a class are paid according to the salary range for that class. One class title covers all of these positions, and they are all tested by the same examination.

B. FOUR BASIC STEPS

1) Study the announcement

How, then, can you know what subjects to study? Our best answer is: "Learn as much as possible about the class of positions for which you've applied." The exam will test the knowledge, skills and abilities needed to do the work.

Your most valuable source of information about the position you want is the official exam announcement. This announcement lists the training and experience qualifications. Check these standards and apply only if you come reasonably close to meeting them.

The brief description of the position in the examination announcement offers some clues to the subjects which will be tested. Think about the job itself. Review the duties in your mind. Can you perform them, or are there some in which you are rusty? Fill in the blank spots in your preparation.

Many jurisdictions preview the written test in the exam announcement by including a section called "Knowledge and Abilities Required," "Scope of the Examination," or some similar heading. Here you will find out specifically what fields will be tested.

2) Review your own background

Once you learn in general what the position is all about, and what you need to know to do the work, ask yourself which subjects you already know fairly well and which need improvement. You may wonder whether to concentrate on improving your strong areas or on building some background in your fields of weakness. When the announcement has specified "some knowledge" or "considerable knowledge," or has used adjectives like "beginning principles of..." or "advanced ... methods," you can get a clue as to the number and difficulty of questions to be asked in any given field. More questions, and hence broader coverage, would be included for those subjects which are more important in the work. Now weigh your strengths and weaknesses against the job requirements and prepare accordingly.

3) Determine the level of the position

Another way to tell how intensively you should prepare is to understand the level of the job for which you are applying. Is it the entering level? In other words, is this the position in which beginners in a field of work are hired? Or is it an intermediate or advanced level? Sometimes this is indicated by such words as "Junior" or "Senior" in the class title. Other jurisdictions use Roman numerals to designate the level – Clerk I, Clerk II, for example. The word "Supervisor" sometimes appears in the title. If the level is not indicated by the title, check the description of duties. Will you be working under very close supervision, or will you have responsibility for independent decisions in this work?

4) Choose appropriate study materials

Now that you know the subjects to be examined and the relative amount of each subject to be covered, you can choose suitable study materials. For beginning level jobs, or even advanced ones, if you have a pronounced weakness in some aspect of your training, read a modern, standard textbook in that field. Be sure it is up to date and has general coverage. Such books are normally available at your library, and the librarian will be glad to help you locate one. For entry-level positions, questions of appropriate difficulty are chosen – neither highly advanced questions, nor those too simple. Such questions require careful thought but not advanced training.

If the position for which you are applying is technical or advanced, you will read more advanced, specialized material. If you are already familiar with the basic principles of your field, elementary textbooks would waste your time. Concentrate on advanced textbooks and technical periodicals. Think through the concepts and review difficult problems in your field.

These are all general sources. You can get more ideas on your own initiative, following these leads. For example, training manuals and publications of the government agency which employs workers in your field can be useful, particularly for technical and professional positions. A letter or visit to the government department involved may result in more specific study suggestions, and certainly will provide you with a more definite idea of the exact nature of the position you are seeking.

III. KINDS OF TESTS

Tests are used for purposes other than measuring knowledge and ability to perform specified duties. For some positions, it is equally important to test ability to make adjustments to new situations or to profit from training. In others, basic mental abilities not dependent on information are essential. Questions which test these things may not appear as pertinent to the duties of the position as those which test for knowledge and information. Yet they are often highly important parts of a fair examination. For very general questions, it is almost impossible to help you direct your study efforts. What we can do is to point out some of the more common of these general abilities needed in public service positions and describe some typical questions.

1) General information

Broad, general information has been found useful for predicting job success in some kinds of work. This is tested in a variety of ways, from vocabulary lists to questions about current events. Basic background in some field of work, such as sociology or economics, may be sampled in a group of questions. Often these are principles which have become familiar to most persons through exposure rather than through formal training. It is difficult to advise you how to study for these questions; being alert to the world around you is our best suggestion.

2) Verbal ability

An example of an ability needed in many positions is verbal or language ability. Verbal ability is, in brief, the ability to use and understand words. Vocabulary and grammar tests are typical measures of this ability. Reading comprehension or paragraph interpretation questions are common in many kinds of civil service tests. You are given a paragraph of written material and asked to find its central meaning.

3) Numerical ability
Number skills can be tested by the familiar arithmetic problem, by checking paired lists of numbers to see which are alike and which are different, or by interpreting charts and graphs. In the latter test, a graph may be printed in the test booklet which you are asked to use as the basis for answering questions.

4) Observation
A popular test for law-enforcement positions is the observation test. A picture is shown to you for several minutes, then taken away. Questions about the picture test your ability to observe both details and larger elements.

5) Following directions
In many positions in the public service, the employee must be able to carry out written instructions dependably and accurately. You may be given a chart with several columns, each column listing a variety of information. The questions require you to carry out directions involving the information given in the chart.

6) Skills and aptitudes
Performance tests effectively measure some manual skills and aptitudes. When the skill is one in which you are trained, such as typing or shorthand, you can practice. These tests are often very much like those given in business school or high school courses. For many of the other skills and aptitudes, however, no short-time preparation can be made. Skills and abilities natural to you or that you have developed throughout your lifetime are being tested.

Many of the general questions just described provide all the data needed to answer the questions and ask you to use your reasoning ability to find the answers. Your best preparation for these tests, as well as for tests of facts and ideas, is to be at your physical and mental best. You, no doubt, have your own methods of getting into an exam-taking mood and keeping "in shape." The next section lists some ideas on this subject.

IV. KINDS OF QUESTIONS

Only rarely is the "essay" question, which you answer in narrative form, used in civil service tests. Civil service tests are usually of the short-answer type. Full instructions for answering these questions will be given to you at the examination. But in case this is your first experience with short-answer questions and separate answer sheets, here is what you need to know:

1) **Multiple-choice Questions**
Most popular of the short-answer questions is the "multiple choice" or "best answer" question. It can be used, for example, to test for factual knowledge, ability to solve problems or judgment in meeting situations found at work.
A multiple-choice question is normally one of three types—
- It can begin with an incomplete statement followed by several possible endings. You are to find the one ending which *best* completes the statement, although some of the others may not be entirely wrong.
- It can also be a complete statement in the form of a question which is answered by choosing one of the statements listed.

- It can be in the form of a problem – again you select the best answer.

Here is an example of a multiple-choice question with a discussion which should give you some clues as to the method for choosing the right answer:

When an employee has a complaint about his assignment, the action which will *best* help him overcome his difficulty is to
- A. discuss his difficulty with his coworkers
- B. take the problem to the head of the organization
- C. take the problem to the person who gave him the assignment
- D. say nothing to anyone about his complaint

In answering this question, you should study each of the choices to find which is best. Consider choice "A" – Certainly an employee may discuss his complaint with fellow employees, but no change or improvement can result, and the complaint remains unresolved. Choice "B" is a poor choice since the head of the organization probably does not know what assignment you have been given, and taking your problem to him is known as "going over the head" of the supervisor. The supervisor, or person who made the assignment, is the person who can clarify it or correct any injustice. Choice "C" is, therefore, correct. To say nothing, as in choice "D," is unwise. Supervisors have and interest in knowing the problems employees are facing, and the employee is seeking a solution to his problem.

2) True/False Questions

The "true/false" or "right/wrong" form of question is sometimes used. Here a complete statement is given. Your job is to decide whether the statement is right or wrong.

SAMPLE: A roaming cell-phone call to a nearby city costs less than a non-roaming call to a distant city.

This statement is wrong, or false, since roaming calls are more expensive.

This is not a complete list of all possible question forms, although most of the others are variations of these common types. You will always get complete directions for answering questions. Be sure you understand *how* to mark your answers – ask questions until you do.

V. RECORDING YOUR ANSWERS

Computer terminals are used more and more today for many different kinds of exams.

For an examination with very few applicants, you may be told to record your answers in the test booklet itself. Separate answer sheets are much more common. If this separate answer sheet is to be scored by machine – and this is often the case – it is highly important that you mark your answers correctly in order to get credit.

An electronic scoring machine is often used in civil service offices because of the speed with which papers can be scored. Machine-scored answer sheets must be marked with a pencil, which will be given to you. This pencil has a high graphite content which responds to the electronic scoring machine. As a matter of fact, stray dots may register as answers, so do not let your pencil rest on the answer sheet while you are pondering the correct answer. Also, if your pencil lead breaks or is otherwise defective, ask for another.

Since the answer sheet will be dropped in a slot in the scoring machine, be careful not to bend the corners or get the paper crumpled.

The answer sheet normally has five vertical columns of numbers, with 30 numbers to a column. These numbers correspond to the question numbers in your test booklet. After each number, going across the page are four or five pairs of dotted lines. These short dotted lines have small letters or numbers above them. The first two pairs may also have a "T" or "F" above the letters. This indicates that the first two pairs only are to be used if the questions are of the true-false type. If the questions are multiple choice, disregard the "T" and "F" and pay attention only to the small letters or numbers.

Answer your questions in the manner of the sample that follows:

32. The largest city in the United States is
    A. Washington, D.C.
    B. New York City
    C. Chicago
    D. Detroit
    E. San Francisco

1) Choose the answer you think is best. (New York City is the largest, so "B" is correct.)
2) Find the row of dotted lines numbered the same as the question you are answering. (Find row number 32)
3) Find the pair of dotted lines corresponding to the answer. (Find the pair of lines under the mark "B.")
4) Make a solid black mark between the dotted lines.

VI. BEFORE THE TEST

Common sense will help you find procedures to follow to get ready for an examination. Too many of us, however, overlook these sensible measures. Indeed, nervousness and fatigue have been found to be the most serious reasons why applicants fail to do their best on civil service tests. Here is a list of reminders:

- Begin your preparation early – Don't wait until the last minute to go scurrying around for books and materials or to find out what the position is all about.
- Prepare continuously – An hour a night for a week is better than an all-night cram session. This has been definitely established. What is more, a night a week for a month will return better dividends than crowding your study into a shorter period of time.
- Locate the place of the exam – You have been sent a notice telling you when and where to report for the examination. If the location is in a different town or otherwise unfamiliar to you, it would be well to inquire the best route and learn something about the building.
- Relax the night before the test – Allow your mind to rest. Do not study at all that night. Plan some mild recreation or diversion; then go to bed early and get a good night's sleep.
- Get up early enough to make a leisurely trip to the place for the test – This way unforeseen events, traffic snarls, unfamiliar buildings, etc. will not upset you.
- Dress comfortably – A written test is not a fashion show. You will be known by number and not by name, so wear something comfortable.

- Leave excess paraphernalia at home – Shopping bags and odd bundles will get in your way. You need bring only the items mentioned in the official notice you received; usually everything you need is provided. Do not bring reference books to the exam. They will only confuse those last minutes and be taken away from you when in the test room.
- Arrive somewhat ahead of time – If because of transportation schedules you must get there very early, bring a newspaper or magazine to take your mind off yourself while waiting.
- Locate the examination room – When you have found the proper room, you will be directed to the seat or part of the room where you will sit. Sometimes you are given a sheet of instructions to read while you are waiting. Do not fill out any forms until you are told to do so; just read them and be prepared.
- Relax and prepare to listen to the instructions
- If you have any physical problem that may keep you from doing your best, be sure to tell the test administrator. If you are sick or in poor health, you really cannot do your best on the exam. You can come back and take the test some other time.

VII. AT THE TEST

The day of the test is here and you have the test booklet in your hand. The temptation to get going is very strong. Caution! There is more to success than knowing the right answers. You must know how to identify your papers and understand variations in the type of short-answer question used in this particular examination. Follow these suggestions for maximum results from your efforts:

1) Cooperate with the monitor

The test administrator has a duty to create a situation in which you can be as much at ease as possible. He will give instructions, tell you when to begin, check to see that you are marking your answer sheet correctly, and so on. He is not there to guard you, although he will see that your competitors do not take unfair advantage. He wants to help you do your best.

2) Listen to all instructions

Don't jump the gun! Wait until you understand all directions. In most civil service tests you get more time than you need to answer the questions. So don't be in a hurry. Read each word of instructions until you clearly understand the meaning. Study the examples, listen to all announcements and follow directions. Ask questions if you do not understand what to do.

3) Identify your papers

Civil service exams are usually identified by number only. You will be assigned a number; you must not put your name on your test papers. Be sure to copy your number correctly. Since more than one exam may be given, copy your exact examination title.

4) Plan your time

Unless you are told that a test is a "speed" or "rate of work" test, speed itself is usually not important. Time enough to answer all the questions will be provided, but this does not mean that you have all day. An overall time limit has been set. Divide the total time (in minutes) by the number of questions to determine the approximate time you have for each question.

5) Do not linger over difficult questions

If you come across a difficult question, mark it with a paper clip (useful to have along) and come back to it when you have been through the booklet. One caution if you do this – be sure to skip a number on your answer sheet as well. Check often to be sure that you have not lost your place and that you are marking in the row numbered the same as the question you are answering.

6) Read the questions

Be sure you know what the question asks! Many capable people are unsuccessful because they failed to *read* the questions correctly.

7) Answer all questions

Unless you have been instructed that a penalty will be deducted for incorrect answers, it is better to guess than to omit a question.

8) Speed tests

It is often better NOT to guess on speed tests. It has been found that on timed tests people are tempted to spend the last few seconds before time is called in marking answers at random – without even reading them – in the hope of picking up a few extra points. To discourage this practice, the instructions may warn you that your score will be "corrected" for guessing. That is, a penalty will be applied. The incorrect answers will be deducted from the correct ones, or some other penalty formula will be used.

9) Review your answers

If you finish before time is called, go back to the questions you guessed or omitted to give them further thought. Review other answers if you have time.

10) Return your test materials

If you are ready to leave before others have finished or time is called, take ALL your materials to the monitor and leave quietly. Never take any test material with you. The monitor can discover whose papers are not complete, and taking a test booklet may be grounds for disqualification.

VIII. EXAMINATION TECHNIQUES

1) Read the general instructions carefully. These are usually printed on the first page of the exam booklet. As a rule, these instructions refer to the timing of the examination; the fact that you should not start work until the signal and must stop work at a signal, etc. If there are any *special* instructions, such as a choice of questions to be answered, make sure that you note this instruction carefully.

2) When you are ready to start work on the examination, that is as soon as the signal has been given, read the instructions to each question booklet, underline any key words or phrases, such as *least, best, outline, describe* and the like. In this way you will tend to answer as requested rather than discover on reviewing your paper that you *listed without describing*, that you selected the *worst* choice rather than the *best* choice, etc.

3) If the examination is of the objective or multiple-choice type – that is, each question will also give a series of possible answers: A, B, C or D, and you are called upon to select the best answer and write the letter next to that answer on your answer paper – it is advisable to start answering each question in turn. There may be anywhere from 50 to 100 such questions in the three or four hours allotted and you can see how much time would be taken if you read through all the questions before beginning to answer any. Furthermore, if you come across a question or group of questions which you know would be difficult to answer, it would undoubtedly affect your handling of all the other questions.

4) If the examination is of the essay type and contains but a few questions, it is a moot point as to whether you should read all the questions before starting to answer any one. Of course, if you are given a choice – say five out of seven and the like – then it is essential to read all the questions so you can eliminate the two that are most difficult. If, however, you are asked to answer all the questions, there may be danger in trying to answer the easiest one first because you may find that you will spend too much time on it. The best technique is to answer the first question, then proceed to the second, etc.

5) Time your answers. Before the exam begins, write down the time it started, then add the time allowed for the examination and write down the time it must be completed, then divide the time available somewhat as follows:
    - If 3-1/2 hours are allowed, that would be 210 minutes. If you have 80 objective-type questions, that would be an average of 2-1/2 minutes per question. Allow yourself no more than 2 minutes per question, or a total of 160 minutes, which will permit about 50 minutes to review.
    - If for the time allotment of 210 minutes there are 7 essay questions to answer, that would average about 30 minutes a question. Give yourself only 25 minutes per question so that you have about 35 minutes to review.

6) The most important instruction is to *read each question* and make sure you know what is wanted. The second most important instruction is to *time yourself properly* so that you answer every question. The third most important instruction is to *answer every question*. Guess if you have to but include something for each question. Remember that you will receive no credit for a blank and will probably receive some credit if you write something in answer to an essay question. If you guess a letter – say "B" for a multiple-choice question – you may have guessed right. If you leave a blank as an answer to a multiple-choice question, the examiners may respect your feelings but it will not add a point to your score. Some exams may penalize you for wrong answers, so in such cases *only*, you may not want to guess unless you have some basis for your answer.

7) Suggestions
    a. Objective-type questions
        1. Examine the question booklet for proper sequence of pages and questions
        2. Read all instructions carefully
        3. Skip any question which seems too difficult; return to it after all other questions have been answered
        4. Apportion your time properly; do not spend too much time on any single question or group of questions

5. Note and underline key words – *all, most, fewest, least, best, worst, same, opposite,* etc.
6. Pay particular attention to negatives
7. Note unusual option, e.g., unduly long, short, complex, different or similar in content to the body of the question
8. Observe the use of "hedging" words – *probably, may, most likely,* etc.
9. Make sure that your answer is put next to the same number as the question
10. Do not second-guess unless you have good reason to believe the second answer is definitely more correct
11. Cross out original answer if you decide another answer is more accurate; do not erase until you are ready to hand your paper in
12. Answer all questions; guess unless instructed otherwise
13. Leave time for review

   b. Essay questions
1. Read each question carefully
2. Determine exactly what is wanted. Underline key words or phrases.
3. Decide on outline or paragraph answer
4. Include many different points and elements unless asked to develop any one or two points or elements
5. Show impartiality by giving pros and cons unless directed to select one side only
6. Make and write down any assumptions you find necessary to answer the questions
7. Watch your English, grammar, punctuation and choice of words
8. Time your answers; don't crowd material

8) Answering the essay question

Most essay questions can be answered by framing the specific response around several key words or ideas. Here are a few such key words or ideas:

M's: manpower, materials, methods, money, management
P's: purpose, program, policy, plan, procedure, practice, problems, pitfalls, personnel, public relations

   a. Six basic steps in handling problems:
1. Preliminary plan and background development
2. Collect information, data and facts
3. Analyze and interpret information, data and facts
4. Analyze and develop solutions as well as make recommendations
5. Prepare report and sell recommendations
6. Install recommendations and follow up effectiveness

   b. Pitfalls to avoid
1. *Taking things for granted* – A statement of the situation does not necessarily imply that each of the elements is necessarily true; for example, a complaint may be invalid and biased so that all that can be taken for granted is that a complaint has been registered

2. *Considering only one side of a situation* – Wherever possible, indicate several alternatives and then point out the reasons you selected the best one
3. *Failing to indicate follow up* – Whenever your answer indicates action on your part, make certain that you will take proper follow-up action to see how successful your recommendations, procedures or actions turn out to be
4. *Taking too long in answering any single question* – Remember to time your answers properly

IX. AFTER THE TEST

Scoring procedures differ in detail among civil service jurisdictions although the general principles are the same. Whether the papers are hand-scored or graded by machine we have described, they are nearly always graded by number. That is, the person who marks the paper knows only the number – never the name – of the applicant. Not until all the papers have been graded will they be matched with names. If other tests, such as training and experience or oral interview ratings have been given, scores will be combined. Different parts of the examination usually have different weights. For example, the written test might count 60 percent of the final grade, and a rating of training and experience 40 percent. In many jurisdictions, veterans will have a certain number of points added to their grades.

After the final grade has been determined, the names are placed in grade order and an eligible list is established. There are various methods for resolving ties between those who get the same final grade – probably the most common is to place first the name of the person whose application was received first. Job offers are made from the eligible list in the order the names appear on it. You will be notified of your grade and your rank as soon as all these computations have been made. This will be done as rapidly as possible.

People who are found to meet the requirements in the announcement are called "eligibles." Their names are put on a list of eligible candidates. An eligible's chances of getting a job depend on how high he stands on this list and how fast agencies are filling jobs from the list.

When a job is to be filled from a list of eligibles, the agency asks for the names of people on the list of eligibles for that job. When the civil service commission receives this request, it sends to the agency the names of the three people highest on this list. Or, if the job to be filled has specialized requirements, the office sends the agency the names of the top three persons who meet these requirements from the general list.

The appointing officer makes a choice from among the three people whose names were sent to him. If the selected person accepts the appointment, the names of the others are put back on the list to be considered for future openings.

That is the rule in hiring from all kinds of eligible lists, whether they are for typist, carpenter, chemist, or something else. For every vacancy, the appointing officer has his choice of any one of the top three eligibles on the list. This explains why the person whose name is on top of the list sometimes does not get an appointment when some of the persons lower on the list do. If the appointing officer chooses the second or third eligible, the No. 1 eligible does not get a job at once, but stays on the list until he is appointed or the list is terminated.

X. HOW TO PASS THE INTERVIEW TEST

The examination for which you applied requires an oral interview test. You have already taken the written test and you are now being called for the interview test – the final part of the formal examination.

You may think that it is not possible to prepare for an interview test and that there are no procedures to follow during an interview. Our purpose is to point out some things you can do in advance that will help you and some good rules to follow and pitfalls to avoid while you are being interviewed.

What is an interview supposed to test?

The written examination is designed to test the technical knowledge and competence of the candidate; the oral is designed to evaluate intangible qualities, not readily measured otherwise, and to establish a list showing the relative fitness of each candidate – as measured against his competitors – for the position sought. Scoring is not on the basis of "right" and "wrong," but on a sliding scale of values ranging from "not passable" to "outstanding." As a matter of fact, it is possible to achieve a relatively low score without a single "incorrect" answer because of evident weakness in the qualities being measured.

Occasionally, an examination may consist entirely of an oral test – either an individual or a group oral. In such cases, information is sought concerning the technical knowledges and abilities of the candidate, since there has been no written examination for this purpose. More commonly, however, an oral test is used to supplement a written examination.

Who conducts interviews?

The composition of oral boards varies among different jurisdictions. In nearly all, a representative of the personnel department serves as chairman. One of the members of the board may be a representative of the department in which the candidate would work. In some cases, "outside experts" are used, and, frequently, a businessman or some other representative of the general public is asked to serve. Labor and management or other special groups may be represented. The aim is to secure the services of experts in the appropriate field.

However the board is composed, it is a good idea (and not at all improper or unethical) to ascertain in advance of the interview who the members are and what groups they represent. When you are introduced to them, you will have some idea of their backgrounds and interests, and at least you will not stutter and stammer over their names.

What should be done before the interview?

While knowledge about the board members is useful and takes some of the surprise element out of the interview, there is other preparation which is more substantive. It *is* possible to prepare for an oral interview – in several ways:

1) Keep a copy of your application and review it carefully before the interview

This may be the only document before the oral board, and the starting point of the interview. Know what education and experience you have listed there, and the sequence and dates of all of it. Sometimes the board will ask you to review the highlights of your experience for them; you should not have to hem and haw doing it.

2) Study the class specification and the examination announcement

Usually, the oral board has one or both of these to guide them. The qualities, characteristics or knowledges required by the position sought are stated in these documents. They offer valuable clues as to the nature of the oral interview. For example, if the job involves supervisory responsibilities, the announcement will usually indicate that knowledge of modern supervisory methods and the qualifications of the candidate as a supervisor will be tested. If so, you can expect such questions, frequently in the form of a hypothetical situation which you are expected to solve. NEVER go into an oral without knowledge of the duties and responsibilities of the job you seek.

3) Think through each qualification required

Try to visualize the kind of questions you would ask if you were a board member. How well could you answer them? Try especially to appraise your own knowledge and background in each area, *measured against the job sought*, and identify any areas in which you are weak. Be critical and realistic – do not flatter yourself.

4) Do some general reading in areas in which you feel you may be weak

For example, if the job involves supervision and your past experience has NOT, some general reading in supervisory methods and practices, particularly in the field of human relations, might be useful. Do NOT study agency procedures or detailed manuals. The oral board will be testing your understanding and capacity, not your memory.

5) Get a good night's sleep and watch your general health and mental attitude

You will want a clear head at the interview. Take care of a cold or any other minor ailment, and of course, no hangovers.

What should be done on the day of the interview?

Now comes the day of the interview itself. Give yourself plenty of time to get there. Plan to arrive somewhat ahead of the scheduled time, particularly if your appointment is in the fore part of the day. If a previous candidate fails to appear, the board might be ready for you a bit early. By early afternoon an oral board is almost invariably behind schedule if there are many candidates, and you may have to wait. Take along a book or magazine to read, or your application to review, but leave any extraneous material in the waiting room when you go in for your interview. In any event, relax and compose yourself.

The matter of dress is important. The board is forming impressions about you – from your experience, your manners, your attitude, and your appearance. Give your personal appearance careful attention. Dress your best, but not your flashiest. Choose conservative, appropriate clothing, and be sure it is immaculate. This is a business interview, and your appearance should indicate that you regard it as such. Besides, being well groomed and properly dressed will help boost your confidence.

Sooner or later, someone will call your name and escort you into the interview room. *This is it.* From here on you are on your own. It is too late for any more preparation. But remember, you asked for this opportunity to prove your fitness, and you are here because your request was granted.

What happens when you go in?

The usual sequence of events will be as follows: The clerk (who is often the board stenographer) will introduce you to the chairman of the oral board, who will introduce you to the other members of the board. Acknowledge the introductions before you sit down. Do not be surprised if you find a microphone facing you or a stenotypist sitting by. Oral interviews are usually recorded in the event of an appeal or other review.

Usually the chairman of the board will open the interview by reviewing the highlights of your education and work experience from your application – primarily for the benefit of the other members of the board, as well as to get the material into the record. Do not interrupt or comment unless there is an error or significant misinterpretation; if that is the case, do not hesitate. But do not quibble about insignificant matters. Also, he will usually ask you some question about your education, experience or your present job – partly to get you to start talking and to establish the interviewing "rapport." He may start the actual questioning, or turn it over to one of the other members. Frequently, each member undertakes the questioning on a particular area, one in which he is perhaps most competent, so you can expect each member to participate in the examination. Because time is limited, you may also expect some rather abrupt switches in the direction the questioning takes, so do not be upset by it. Normally, a board member will not pursue a single line of questioning unless he discovers a particular strength or weakness.

After each member has participated, the chairman will usually ask whether any member has any further questions, then will ask you if you have anything you wish to add. Unless you are expecting this question, it may floor you. Worse, it may start you off on an extended, extemporaneous speech. The board is not usually seeking more information. The question is principally to offer you a last opportunity to present further qualifications or to indicate that you have nothing to add. So, if you feel that a significant qualification or characteristic has been overlooked, it is proper to point it out in a sentence or so. Do not compliment the board on the thoroughness of their examination – they have been sketchy, and you know it. If you wish, merely say, "No thank you, I have nothing further to add." This is a point where you can "talk yourself out" of a good impression or fail to present an important bit of information. Remember, *you close the interview yourself*.

The chairman will then say, "That is all, Mr. _____, thank you." Do not be startled; the interview is over, and quicker than you think. Thank him, gather your belongings and take your leave. Save your sigh of relief for the other side of the door.

How to put your best foot forward

Throughout this entire process, you may feel that the board individually and collectively is trying to pierce your defenses, seek out your hidden weaknesses and embarrass and confuse you. Actually, this is not true. They are obliged to make an appraisal of your qualifications for the job you are seeking, and they want to see you in your best light. Remember, they must interview all candidates and a non-cooperative candidate may become a failure in spite of their best efforts to bring out his qualifications. Here are 15 suggestions that will help you:

1) Be natural – Keep your attitude confident, not cocky

If you are not confident that you can do the job, do not expect the board to be. Do not apologize for your weaknesses, try to bring out your strong points. The board is interested in a positive, not negative, presentation. Cockiness will antagonize any board member and make him wonder if you are covering up a weakness by a false show of strength.

2) Get comfortable, but don't lounge or sprawl

Sit erectly but not stiffly. A careless posture may lead the board to conclude that you are careless in other things, or at least that you are not impressed by the importance of the occasion. Either conclusion is natural, even if incorrect. Do not fuss with your clothing, a pencil or an ashtray. Your hands may occasionally be useful to emphasize a point; do not let them become a point of distraction.

3) Do not wisecrack or make small talk

This is a serious situation, and your attitude should show that you consider it as such. Further, the time of the board is limited – they do not want to waste it, and neither should you.

4) Do not exaggerate your experience or abilities
In the first place, from information in the application or other interviews and sources, the board may know more about you than you think. Secondly, you probably will not get away with it. An experienced board is rather adept at spotting such a situation, so do not take the chance.

5) If you know a board member, do not make a point of it, yet do not hide it
Certainly you are not fooling him, and probably not the other members of the board. Do not try to take advantage of your acquaintanceship – it will probably do you little good.

6) Do not dominate the interview
Let the board do that. They will give you the clues – do not assume that you have to do all the talking. Realize that the board has a number of questions to ask you, and do not try to take up all the interview time by showing off your extensive knowledge of the answer to the first one.

7) Be attentive
You only have 20 minutes or so, and you should keep your attention at its sharpest throughout. When a member is addressing a problem or question to you, give him your undivided attention. Address your reply principally to him, but do not exclude the other board members.

8) Do not interrupt
A board member may be stating a problem for you to analyze. He will ask you a question when the time comes. Let him state the problem, and wait for the question.

9) Make sure you understand the question
Do not try to answer until you are sure what the question is. If it is not clear, restate it in your own words or ask the board member to clarify it for you. However, do not haggle about minor elements.

10) Reply promptly but not hastily
A common entry on oral board rating sheets is "candidate responded readily," or "candidate hesitated in replies." Respond as promptly and quickly as you can, but do not jump to a hasty, ill-considered answer.

11) Do not be peremptory in your answers
A brief answer is proper – but do not fire your answer back. That is a losing game from your point of view. The board member can probably ask questions much faster than you can answer them.

12) Do not try to create the answer you think the board member wants
He is interested in what kind of mind you have and how it works – not in playing games. Furthermore, he can usually spot this practice and will actually grade you down on it.

13) Do not switch sides in your reply merely to agree with a board member
Frequently, a member will take a contrary position merely to draw you out and to see if you are willing and able to defend your point of view. Do not start a debate, yet do not surrender a good position. If a position is worth taking, it is worth defending.

14) Do not be afraid to admit an error in judgment if you are shown to be wrong

The board knows that you are forced to reply without any opportunity for careful consideration. Your answer may be demonstrably wrong. If so, admit it and get on with the interview.

15) Do not dwell at length on your present job

The opening question may relate to your present assignment. Answer the question but do not go into an extended discussion. You are being examined for a *new* job, not your present one. As a matter of fact, try to phrase ALL your answers in terms of the job for which you are being examined.

Basis of Rating

Probably you will forget most of these "do's" and "don'ts" when you walk into the oral interview room. Even remembering them all will not ensure you a passing grade. Perhaps you did not have the qualifications in the first place. But remembering them will help you to put your best foot forward, without treading on the toes of the board members.

Rumor and popular opinion to the contrary notwithstanding, an oral board wants you to make the best appearance possible. They know you are under pressure – but they also want to see how you respond to it as a guide to what your reaction would be under the pressures of the job you seek. They will be influenced by the degree of poise you display, the personal traits you show and the manner in which you respond.

ABOUT THIS BOOK

This book contains tests divided into Examination Sections. Go through each test, answering every question in the margin. We have also attached a sample answer sheet at the back of the book that can be removed and used. At the end of each test look at the answer key and check your answers. On the ones you got wrong, look at the right answer choice and learn. Do not fill in the answers first. Do not memorize the questions and answers, but understand the answer and principles involved. On your test, the questions will likely be different from the samples. Questions are changed and new ones added. If you understand these past questions you should have success with any changes that arise. Tests may consist of several types of questions. We have additional books on each subject should more study be advisable or necessary for you. Finally, the more you study, the better prepared you will be. This book is intended to be the last thing you study before you walk into the examination room. Prior study of relevant texts is also recommended. NLC publishes some of these in our Fundamental Series. Knowledge and good sense are important factors in passing your exam. Good luck also helps. So now study this Passbook, absorb the material contained within and take that knowledge into the examination. Then do your best to pass that exam.

EXAMINATION SECTION

EXAMINATION SECTION
TEST 1

DIRECTIONS: Each question or incomplete statement is followed by several suggested answers or completions. Select the one that BEST answers the question or completes the statement. *PRINT THE LETTER OF THE CORRECT ANSWER IN THE SPACE AT THE RIGHT.*

1. Assume you are a housing inspector assigned to make an inspection of an apartment house.
   The MOST desirable procedure to follow is:

   A. Before beginning this inspection, you should make an appointment with the owner so that he may have a representative present when you arrive
   B. You should make your inspection without revealing your identity
   C. You should reveal your identity only if challenged
   D. Upon arrival at the premises, you should identify yourself to the owner or his representative before proceeding with your inspection

1.____

2. Suppose that you were preparing a report on your investigation of a tenant complaint. Of the following, the item that you should consider LEAST necessary for inclusion in your report is the

   A. height of the building
   B. address of the building
   C. specific violations discovered
   D. name of the complaining tenant

2.____

3. During an inspection of a tenant's apartment, you are asked for information about enforcement of orders to correct violations.
   Of the following, the MOST proper reply to the tenant is to

   A. advise the tenant to write a letter to Department headquarters so that his inquiry can be treated as an official matter
   B. refuse to tell the tenant anything since this is a matter between the owner and the Department
   C. explain briefly the usual procedure in connection with the processing of complaints in your Department
   D. advise the tenant to withhold rent payment until the violations found in her apartment are removed

3.____

Questions 4-7.

DIRECTIONS: Questions 4 through 7 are to be answered on the basis of the following situation.

   Assume you are an Inspector of Housing. While investigating a complaint about broken plaster, the tenant who made the complaint tells you that the building is vermin- and rat-infested. Your inspection shows the plaster to be in very unsatisfactory condition, but you see no evidence of vermin or rats. The tenant tells you that vermin and rats appear only in the evening. The apartment is kept in a very slovenly manner.

4. Of the following statements, the MOST important one to include in your report in addition to your findings regarding the plaster is:

   A. The apartment is slovenly kept
   B. The apartment is not vermin- and rat-infested
   C. the tenant said the apartment was infested
   D. there was no evidence of vermin- or rat-infestation as the tenant had claimed

5. In making your investigation, you should be

   A. very short with the tenant
   B. very loquacious so that you encourage the tenant to tell you about other violations
   C. very polite and agree with everything the tenant says
   D. pleasant but discourage undue conversation

6. With regard to the slovenly way in which the apartment is kept, you should

   A. make no mention of it to the tenant
   B. point out to the tenant that he does not deserve to have the plaster fixed
   C. be diplomatic by pointing out that it will be easier to keep the apartment clean when the plaster is fixed
   D. tell the tenant that dirt breeds vermin and it would be a good idea for him to start cleaning up

7. Assume that the Department requires reports to be made on a blank card.
   Of the following, the BEST statement to enter on your card concerning your findings is:

   A. Complaint exaggerated but there is a violation
   B. Inspected Apt. 2B at 700 West 400th Street and found wall plaster badly cracked with several breaks showing lath in all rooms
   C. Inspected Apt. 2B at 700 West 400th Street. Violations exist.
   D. Inspected Apt. 2B at 700 West 400th Street. Found plaster badly cracked and broken in some rooms.

8. Of the following equipment, the item that is LEAST likely to be required by an Inspector of Housing on a routine inspection is a

   A. 6' rule   B. 25' tape
   C. flashlight   D. notebook

9. According to the Multiple Dwelling Law, in all new-law-tenements there shall be access to every living room and bedroom and to at least one bathroom without passing through any bedroom.
   Of the following, the MOST important reason for this requirement is that it

   A. provides better ventilation of apartments
   B. assures privacy to occupants
   C. reduces fire and health hazards
   D. improves the arrangement of rooms of apartments

10. While investigating a complaint of a condition not dangerous or detrimental to life or health, an inspector is asked by the complainant, a tenant, if this condition constitutes a violation.
    Of the following, the MOST acceptable answer is:

    A. It is none of your business
    B. Yes. We will take him into court immediately.
    C. Yes. We will notify him of the violation immediately and the condition will be corrected in a few days or we will prosecute.
    D. Yes. The landlord will be notified and allowed a reasonable period in which to correct the condition.

11. While making an inspection in the apartment of a tenant, you are informed by him that the janitor makes minor repairs only when he is tipped.
    Of the following, the MOST appropriate action you should take upon receipt of this information is to

    A. discuss the matter of tipping with the owner of the building
    B. advise the janitor that required repairs must be made regardless of the receipt of a gratuity
    C. tell the tenant to discuss the matter with the owner of the building
    D. ask for more information as to the existence of neglected defects in the building

12. Your supervisor asks you to make a re-inspection of a building which you know was recently inspected by a fellow inspector. You are told that this assignment is confidential and is not to be discussed with anyone.
    Of the following, the MOST desirable action to take is to

    A. advise your superior that you do not want to check up on the work of another inspector
    B. discuss the assignment with the other inspector before going out on the inspection
    C. accept the assignment and follow the instructions of your supervisor without comment
    D. insist that you be permitted to see the report of the other inspector before accepting the assignment

Question 13.

DIRECTIONS: Question 13 is to be answered on the basis of the following statement.

When the lot of such a dwelling abuts upon two or more streets, and the difference in level between the highest and the lowest points of the curbs adjoining the lot is more than ten feet, a room below the highest curb point may be used for living purposes provided it opens upon a street or upon a lawful court or yard which connects directly with a street or, if the floor of such a room is not more than twelve feet below the highest curb point, upon an interior court with a least dimension of not less than thirty feet if such court is situated on a lot line.

13. According to the above statement, it is CORRECT to say that

    A. the room described as acceptable for living purposes must in all instances open on a court or yard connecting directly with a street
    B. if the floor of the room is less than twelve feet below the highest curb point, it may not be used for living purposes
    C. no room in such a dwelling may be used for living purposes if the difference in curb points is less than ten feet
    D. a room whose floor is more than twelve feet below
    E. the highest curb point may be used for living purposes if it opens upon a street

Questions 14-15.

DIRECTIONS: Questions 14 and 15 are to be answered on the basis of the following statement.

Whatever is dangerous to human life or detrimental to health, and whatever dwelling is overcrowded with occupants or is not provided with adequate ingress or egress or is not sufficiently supported, ventilated, sewered, drained, cleaned, or lighted in reference to its intended or actual use, and whatever renders the air or human food or drink unwholesome are nuisances. All such nuisances are unlawful.

14. According to the above paragraph,

    A. dwellings with more occupants than one per room are dangerous and are nuisances
    B. dwellings may be considered overcrowded when there is inadequate ingress or egress
    C. if a dwelling is untenanted, it cannot be considered a nuisance under this paragraph
    D. a dwelling may be considered a nuisance if the number of exits from the building is insufficient

15. The word *ingress,* as used in the above paragraph, means MOST NEARLY

    A. entrance   B. water supply
    C. recess   D. water closet

16. Existing cubicles complying with other provisions of this section may be maintained.
    In this sentence, the word *cubicles* means MOST NEARLY

    A. exceptions   B. aisles or halls
    C. party walls   D. enclosed sections

17. An officer or employee of the Department shall be free from liability for acts done by him in good faith in the performance of his official duties.
    In this sentence, the word *liability* means MOST NEARLY

    A. responsibility   B. personal damages
    C. compliance   D. necessary insurance

18. Encumbrances of any kind are forbidden on fire escapes. The word *encumbrances*, as used in this sentence, means MOST NEARLY

    A. braces
    B. shackles
    C. attachments
    D. obstructions

19. If more than one dormer faces a street, their aggregate frontage at any level shall not exceed the frontage length herein permitted at such level.
    The word *aggregate,* as used in this sentence, means MOST NEARLY

    A. total
    B. individual
    C. excess
    D. permitted

20. The location and design of all buildings and structures on the plot shall be consistent with the predominantly residential character of the district.
    The word *predominantly*, as used in this sentence, means MOST NEARLY

    A. prepared
    B. approximate
    C. prevailing
    D. predetermined

Questions 21-24.

DIRECTIONS: In answering Questions 21 through 24, choose the term in Column II MOST closely identified with the item in Column I. Each term may be used more than once or not at all.

COLUMN I

21. Scratch coat
22. Flashing
23. Parapet
24. Newel

COLUMN II

A. Roofing
B. Stair building
C. Plastering
D. Plumbing
E. Painting

25. Of the following, the term which is LEAST related to the others is

    A. ground
    B. lath
    C. plaster
    D. ledger board

26. The upright finished board in the side of a door opening is called a

    A. batten   B. saddle   C. jamb   D. stile

27. Which one of the following terms is LEAST related to the others?

    A. Stop   B. Jamb   C. Buck   D. Siding

28. Which one of the following terms is LEAST related to the others?

    A. Pipe   B. Riser   C. Tread   D. Nosing

29. Of the following terms, the one which is LEAST related to the others is

   A. baseboard B. base mold
   C. casing   D. base plate

30. A ribband or ribbon is a horizontal strip of wood notched into the studs. It is used ONLY in _____-frame construction.

   A. balloon   B. braced   C. platform   D. Western

31. The bracing between wood floor beams is called

   A. internal bracing   B. bridging
   C. reinforcing   D. cross-bracing

32. The MAXIMUM allowable spacing for the bracing described in Question 31 above, according to the City Building Code, is

   A. 6'   B. 8'   C. 10'   D. 12'

33. In wooden floor construction, the bracing described in Question 31 above is used PRIMARILY to

   A. prevent the joists from turning over before the flooring is placed
   B. transfer load from the joist directly under a load on the floor to adjacent joists
   C. keep a uniform spacing of the joists
   D. eliminate the need for header and trimmer beams at floor openings

34. In floor construction, the bracing described in Question 31 above should

   A. be nailed at the top and the lower ends left loose until the sub-flooring is nailed in position
   B. be nailed at both ends before the sub-flooring is placed in position
   C. not be nailed at all until after the sub-flooring is nailed in position
   D. not be nailed until after the sub-flooring is nailed and the finished flooring placed

35. The timbers that support the rough flooring are called

   A. lintels   B. sills   C. beams   D. studs

36. Wood for the wearing surface of a floor should PREFERABLY be

   A. flat-sawed   B. quarter-sawed
   C. cross-cut   D. rip-sawed

37. Wainscoting is

   A. the moulding around a room for hanging pictures
   B. the moulding around a room to protect the plaster from the backs of chairs
   C. panel work covering part or all of a wall
   D. the tile or cement flooring in a kitchen around the stove or range

38. The small bars separating the panes of glass in a panelled window are

   A. rails   B. muntins   C. moldings   D. mullions

39. An extra window, hung over a window of a building, to help keep out wind and cold is a(n) _____ window. 39._____

   A. storm
   B. casement
   C. oriel
   D. double-hung

Questions 40-44.

DIRECTIONS: In Questions 40 through 44, for each figure in Column I, representing a cross-section of a piece of lumber, select the letter preceding the term in Column II which is MOST closely associated with figure. NOTE: These figures are not to scale.

COLUMN I   COLUMN II

40.   A. Flooring   40._____

41.   B. Siding

   C. Baseboard

   D. Window steel

42.   E. Threshold   41._____

   F. Shingle

43.   42._____

44.   43._____

44._____

45. A dry well   45._____

   A. provides drainage without the use of a sewer
   B. is a reservoir for storage of drainage water until such time as the flooded sewer is able to carry this water
   C. is an auxiliary cesspool
   D. provides an approved storage space for rubbish

46. A wall of a building which supports any load other than its own weight is called a _____ wall.

   A. curtain   B. retaining   C. parapet   D. bearing

47. Soffits are USUALLY located in

   A. the roofing
   B. bathrooms
   C. stairways
   D. the flooring

48. Piles are used in building construction

   A. to provide waterproof construction
   B. to eliminate the need for a cellar
   C. when the building is located on sloping ground
   D. to help support the foundation

49. Employees of the department are not permitted to engage in any activity connected with construction, alteration, or equipment of buildings PRIMARILY because

   A. they are required to work fulltime for the city
   B. their employment with the city might give them unfair advantage over others in the same activity who were not employed by the city
   C. such activity might influence their enforcement of the law
   D. they would tend to specialize in a phase of their work in the department which concerned their outside activity, to the detriment of other phases

50. Of the following, the MOST acceptable reason for the enforcement of the Building Code and Multiple Dwelling Law is:

   A. Since all builders are governed by a single code of practice, no builder will have any advantage over any other builder
   B. Minimum standards of safety and comfort are assured for the occupants of buildings
   C. It stimulates the growth of undeveloped sections of the city
   D. It prevents the decline of real estate values

KEY (CORRECT ANSWERS)

1. D	11. C	21. C	31. B	41. D
2. A	12. C	22. A	32. B	42. E
3. C	13. D	23. A	33. B	43. A
4. D	14. D	24. B	34. A	44. B
5. D	15. A	25. D	35. C	45. A
6. A	16. D	26. C	36. B	46. D
7. B	17. B	27. D	37. C	47. C
8. B	18. D	28. A	38. B	48. D
9. B	19. A	29. D	39. A	49. C
10. D	20. C	30. A	40. C	50. B

TEST 2

DIRECTIONS: Each question or incomplete statement is followed by several suggested answers or completions. Select the one that BEST answers the question or completes the statement. *PRINT THE LETTER OF THE CORRECT ANSWER IN THE SPACE AT THE RIGHT.*

1. In determining the dimensions of a rectangular court, a surveyor measured the width as 12'0"; but instead of measuring the depth, measured the length of a diagonal as 20'0". The depth of the court, in feet, is

   A. 18   B. 16   C. 14   D. 12

   1._____

2. Assuming that 6 sq. ft. are allowed per person, the capacity of an assembly hall that is 45 feet wide at the front, 60 feet wide at the rear (front and rear walls parallel), and 75 feet long is MOST NEARLY

   A. 600   B. 650   C. 700   D. 750

   2._____

3. The volume of a rectangular room is 1063 3/4 cu. ft. It is 10'0" and 9'3" wide. Its length is MOST NEARLY

   A. 11'0"   B. 11'3"   C. 11'6"   D. 11'9"

   3._____

4. Seven hundred twenty (720) reports are to be checked. Inspector X can do this job alone in 6 days. Inspector Y, less experienced, can do the job in 10 days. To expedite the work, both inspectors are assigned to share the work in such manner that they will both require the same time for completion.
   The number of reports that Y will check is MOST NEARLY

   A. 270   B. 288   C. 312   D. 330

   4._____

5. In a C district, a building may occupy 60% of the area of a lot.
   If a lot measures 30' x 100', the maximum permissible length of a rectangular building 25 feet wide is MOST NEARLY

   A. 66'   B. 68'   C. 70'   D. 72'

   5._____

6. A room measures 9' x 12'. The light fixture is located in the center of the ceiling.
   The distance from a corner of the room to the center of the light fixture, measured along the ceiling, is MOST NEARLY

   A. 6'6"   B. 7'0"   C. 7'6"   D. 8'0"

   6._____

7. In a class one district, no building shall be erected to a height in excess of 7/8 times the width of the street; but for each one foot that the building or a portion of it sets back from the street line, 1 1/2 feet shall be added to the height limit of such building or such portion thereof.
   According to the above statement, the maximum height of a building in a class one district on a street 100 feet wide where the building is set back 4 feet from the street line is MOST NEARLY

   A. 93'   B. 87'   C. 112'   D. 76'

   7._____

9

8. An old law tenement is one that was constructed before   8.____

   A. April 18, 1929   B. April 15, 1887
   C. April 18, 1912   D. April 12, 1901

9. Of the following, the type of building which is NOT covered by the provisions of the Multi-   9.____
   ple Dwelling Law is a

   A. converted dwelling   B. two-family dwelling
   C. hotel   D. clubhouse

10. According to the City Administrative Code, the power to regulate and limit the height and   10.____
    bulk of buildings and to regulate and determine the areas of yards, courts, and other
    open spaces is delegated to the

    A. Department of Housing and Buildings
    B. City Planning Commission
    C. Board of Standards and Appeals
    D. City Council

11. The regulations of the department with respect to lodging houses do NOT cover   11.____

    A. cleanliness of sheets and pillowcases
    B. amount of space per bed
    C. hours of use of beds by lodgers
    D. fire-retarding of cooking spaces used by lodgers

12. The Multiple Dwelling Law requires the landlord of a tenement to   12.____

    A. provide a resident janitor for the building if it is occupied by six or more families
    B. have previous coats of wallpaper removed before new wallpaper can be applied
    C. paint walls of halls and stairs every three years or less
    D. keep bulkhead doors and scuttles locked with a key lock at all times

13. The MINIMUM sized light, in watts, required in halls and stairs of multiple dwellings,   13.____
    according to the Multiple Dwelling Law, is

    A. 15   B. 30   C. 40   D. 60

14. Of the following, the type of building which may NOT be erected in a residence district is   14.____

    A. railroad passenger station
    B. hospital
    C. bank building
    D. philanthropic institution

15. A fireproof building   15.____

    A. is fire-retarded
    B. must be fire-stopped
    C. must be constructed entirely of incombustible material
    D. is a fire-protected structure

16. Of the following items relating to fire escapes, the one that is NOT permitted, according to the Multiple Dwelling Law, is

    A. balconies
    B. gooseneck ladders
    C. vertical ladder fire escapes
    D. drop ladder

17. A certificate of occupancy is issued by the

    A. Commissioner of Housing and Buildings
    B. Deputy Commissioner of Housing
    C. Deputy Commissioner of Buildings
    D. Borough Superintendent

18. The structure above the roof of a building enclosing a stairway is described by the building code as a(n)

    A. scuttle   B. extension
    C. penthouse   D. bulkhead

19. When a structure containing a party wall is demolished, protection for the party wall is specified by the Building Code.
    Of the following items relating to such protection, the one that is NOT specified by the Code is

    A. the owner of the building being demolished must pay for protecting the party wall
    B. the anchors at the beam ends in the standing wall shall be bent over
    C. the party wall shall be shored up and made secure
    D. all open beam holes shall be bricked in

20. According to the Multiple Dwelling Law, the MINIMUM area of a bedroom in newly constructed Class A multiple dwellings is_____ sq. ft.

    A. 132   B. 116   C. 100   D. 80

21. The height of a room, for the purpose of determining compliance with requirements of the Multiple Dwelling Law, shall be measured from the

    A. top of the floor beams to the bottom of the ceiling beams
    B. center of the floor beams to the center of the ceiling beams
    C. finished floor to the finished ceiling
    D. rough flooring to the finished ceiling

22. The outside temperature below which heat must be supplied to tenants of centrally heated buildings during the day is

    A. 32° F   B. 60° F   C. 55° F   D. 45° F

23. A wiped joint is MOST likely to be found in_____ piping.

    A. vitrified clay sewer   B. cast iron sewer
    C. steel water   D. lead

24. A caulked joint is MOST likely to be found in

    A. vitrified clay sewer piping
    B. bell and spiget metal piping
    C. brass water piping
    D. a connection between a brass pipe and a lead pipe

25. Of the following materials, the one that the city building code does NOT permit for use in underground piping is _____ pipe.

    A. wrought iron
    B. cast iron
    C. lead
    D. brass

26. The drainage system of a building is that part of the plumbing system which receives, conveys, and removes

    A. the discharge of any fixture except water closets
    B. storm water only
    C. liquid and water carried wastes and storm water
    D. the discharge of water closets only

27. The purpose of a trap in a plumbing system is to

    A. provide a means of cleaning out a clogged drain
    B. prevent back syphonage
    C. provide a means of venting the plumbing system
    D. prevent the passage of air or gas through a pipe or fixture

28. Of the following piping, the one that can NOT be termed a stack is _____ piping.

    A. soil
    B. house drain
    C. vent
    D. waste

29. The roughing-in of plumbing constitutes

    A. delivery of plumbing supplies to the site of a building
    B. the installation of the piping
    C. the installation of the plumbing fixtures
    D. the testing of the plumbing

30. Hydrated lime is

    A. lime mixed in mortar
    B. quick lime
    C. pre-slaked lime
    D. waterproof lime

31. A concrete mix is tested for slump to indicate its

    A. freshness
    B. water content
    C. plasticity
    D. strength

32. Rock wool is used in buildings MAINLY to

    A. increase the fire resistive qualities of the walls
    B. act as an insulator of heat in walls
    C. form a barrier against vermin or rodent travel in walls
    D. reduce moisture or condensation on wall surfaces

33. Hair is added to plaster in order to

    A. delay the time of set
    B. make it more workable
    C. bond the finish coat to the brown coat
    D. increase its strength

34. A terrazzo-finish floor consists of

    A. cement, sand, and gravel ground to a smooth finish
    B. cement, sand, and marble chips
    C. tile squares set in fresh mortar
    D. asphaltic tiles set in asphaltic cement

35. A 1:2:4 concrete contains one sack of cement(,)

    A. two cubic feet of sand, and four cubic feet of gravel
    B. two gallons of water, and four cubic feet of aggregate
    C. two wheelbarrows of sand, and four wheelbarrows of gravel
    D. to four cubic feet of aggregate

Questions 86-90.

DIRECTIONS: In answering Questions 86 through 90, choose the term in Column II MOST closely identified with the item in Column I. Each term may be used more than once or not at all.

COLUMN I	COLUMN II
36. Wane	A. Carpentry
37. Parging	B. Plumbing
	C. Masonry
38. Smoke test	D. Riveting
	E. Welding
39. Mortise	F. Plastering
40. Struck joint	G. Roofing

41. In brick work, a bat is

    A. never used in laying up a brick wall
    B. sometimes used so that it appears to be a header
    C. a bonding unit
    D. a stretcher

42. When painting, nail holes and cracks should be

    A. filled with putty before starting
    B. filled with putty after the priming coat is applied
    C. filled with paint by careful working
    D. ignored

43. The white deposit on a new brick wall is due to 43.____

   A. efflorescence B. slaking
   C. sedimentation D. condensation

44. Wire glass is used MAINLY where 44.____

   A. light is required but it is desired to obscure the view
   B. fire-retarding qualities are required
   C. strength is required without the extra cost of heavy plate glass
   D. a diffused light is required

45. Glazier's points are used to 45.____

   A. hold glass in wooden window sash
   B. scratch glass so that it can be broken to size
   C. force putty into narrow spaces between glass and sash
   D. remove broken glass from a pane

46. When pipes are to be hung from the ceilings of a concrete building, it is GOOD practice 46.____
    to provide in the construction

   A. inserts   B. nailing strips
   C. lag screws   D. clamps

47. A good flashing 47.____

   A. is as narrow as possible
   B. usually requires periodic painting
   C. never requires counter-flashing
   D. may be copper or zinc

48. The PRIMARY reason for using headers in brickwork is to 48.____

   A. obtain a particular architectural effect
   B. make a stronger wall
   C. have all bricklayers follow the same pattern
   D. permit easier pointing

49. The process of filling the joints of masonry with mortar and pressing the mortar into the 49.____
    joints is called

   A. grouting   B. buttering
   C. pointing   D. caulking

50. Dwellings may be located on a sanitary landfill. Such landfill that is young in age may 50.____
    present certain hazards. Of the following, the one that is NOT such a hazard is

   A. spontaneous combustion
   B. explosion of combustible gases
   C. contamination of water supply
   D. excavating for utilities may result in the release of bad odors

KEY (CORRECT ANSWERS)

1. B	11. D	21. C	31. C	41. B
2. B	12. B	22. C	32. B	42. B
3. C	13. A	23. D	33. D	43. A
4. A	14. C	24. B	34. B	44. B
5. D	15. D	25. A	35. A	45. A
6. C	16. C	26. C	36. A	46. A
7. A	17. D	27. D	37. C	47. D
8. D	18. D	28. B	38. B	48. B
9. B	19. C	29. B	39. A	49. C
10. B	20. D	30. C	40. C	50. C

EXAMINATION SECTION
TEST 1

DIRECTIONS: Each question or incomplete statement is followed by several suggested answers or completions. Select the one that BEST answers the question or completes the statement. *PRINT THE LETTER OF THE CORRECT ANSWER IN THE SPACE AT THE RIGHT.*

1. A kitchenette is defined as a cooking space having a floor area of LESS than _____ square feet.

    A. 57 B. 58 C. 59 D. 60

2. The one of the following that is classed as a converted dwelling is a(n)

    A. apartment house erected prior to 1929, now used as a hotel
    B. lodging house erected prior to 1913, now used as a multiple dwelling
    C. one-family house erected prior to 1929, now used as a multiple dwelling
    D. rooming house erected prior to 1913, now used as a hotel

3. A *fire-retarded* partition must have a fire-resistive rating of AT LEAST _____ hour(s).

    A. 1 B. 2 C. 3 D. 4

4. The multiple dwelling law states that the total window area of a room must be at least one-tenth of the floor surface area of the room.
The one of the following types of rooms that is exempted from this provision is a

    A. bedroom B. kitchen
    C. recreation room D. bathroom

5. In a non-fireproof multiple dwelling, the HIGHEST story in which a factory may be operated is the

    A. 1st B. 2nd C. 3rd D. 4th

6. In a multiple dwelling under construction, the MINIMUM required width of an entrance hall, from the entrance to the first stair, is

    A. 3'4" B. 3'8" C. 4'0" D. 4'4"

7. Access to a required fire escape, used as a legal second means of egress from an apartment, may be from a

    A. public hall B. kitchen
    C. bathroom D. closet

8. The basis for differentiating between a *tenement* and any other *Class A multiple dwelling* is

    A. the year in which it was built
    B. the number of families now residing therein
    C. whether residents are permanent or transient
    D. classification of construction

9. In a 6-story multiple dwelling under construction, wood floor joists would NOT be used for   9.____

    A. apartments   B. recreation rooms
    C. toilets   D. public halls

10. If plans were to be filed now for a change of occupancy, the type of occupancy for which   10.____
a fire escape is NOT acceptable as a second means of egress is

    A. club house   B. single room
    C. tenement   D. garden type maisonette

11. The multiple dwelling law requires self-closing doors between apartments and halls in all   11.____
Class A multiple dwellings.
The PRINCIPAL reason for this is to

    A. insure privacy of the tenants
    B. protect other tenants from excessive noise
    C. reduce heat loss
    D. prevent the spread of fire

12. The multiple dwelling law prohibits the erection of a building the height of which is in   12.____
excess of one and one-half times the width of the widest street on which it faces.
The MAIN reason for this prohibition is to

    A. insure that tenants will not have to travel too far to the street in case of fire
    B. provide adequate light and air
    C. prevent excessive loadings on the footings
    D. provide adequate water pressure on the top floor

13. The multiple dwelling law requires that the walls of all interior courts shall be built with a   13.____
light-colored brick. The PRINCIPAL reason for this is that

    A. light-colored brick is easier to clean
    B. more light will be reflected into the apartments
    C. light-colored brick is usually stronger
    D. rain will not penetrate light-colored brick readily

14. The multiple dwelling law requires that every fire escape constructed of material subject   14.____
to rusting shall be painted with two or more coats of paint of contrasting colors.
The reason that each coat is required to be of a different color is that

    A. the different pigments in the two coats will better protect the steel from rust
    B. when two colors are used, the sun will not bleach the top color as rapidly as when only one color is used
    C. the contrasting colors make inspection easier
    D. a better bond is obtained between paint of different color

15. The multiple dwelling law requires that every fire escape at the top story of a building   15.____
shall be provided with a stairway or ladder to the roof, except where the roof is a peak roof with a pitch in excess of twenty degrees. The reason that access to the roof from the fire escape is NOT required where the pitch of the roof is in excess of twenty degrees is that

    A. it would be difficult to walk on a roof with such a slope
    B. a steep roof would tend to catch fire quicker, so people should not be on the roof

C. sparks from a fire would tend to roll down the roof toward any person climbing up the ladder
D. it is almost impossible to anchor a ladder to a steep roof

16. The multiple dwelling law states that for stairs, each tread shall be not less than nine and one-half inches wide; each riser shall not exceed seven and three-quarters inches in height; and the product of the number of inches in the width of the tread and the number of inches in the height of the riser shall be at least seventy and at most seventy-five.
The one of the following sets of dimensions that is acceptable for the stairs of a multiple dwelling is tread _____, riser _____.

  A. 9 3/4"; 7 1/8"   B. 9 1/4"; 8"
  C. 10 1/4"; 7 1/8"   D. 10 1/2"; 7 1/2"

17. The multiple dwelling law prohibits construction of a frame multiple dwelling.
The PRINCIPAL reason for this is that

  A. frame buildings are more susceptible to vermin infection
  B. the heavier loads occurring in multiple dwellings can not be supported in frame buildings
  C. frame buildings, used as multiple dwellings, tend to become slums
  D. fire in a frame building is more dangerous than in other types of buildings

18. The multiple dwelling law states that no radio or other wires shall be attached to any vent line extending above the roof.
The PRINCIPAL reason for this prohibition is that

  A. vent lines are relatively weak structures
  B. wires increase the danger of electric shock due to lightning
  C. low wires are a safety hazard
  D. ventilation will be blocked

19. In a non-fireproof building, the multiple dwelling law requires that certain partitions shall be fire-stopped. This means that

  A. fireproof doors must be used
  B. the partitions must be constructed of incombustible material
  C. the covering of the studs must be of incombustible material
  D. the spaces between the top of a partition and the ceiling and floors above must be filled with incombustible material

20. The building code states that the floor of a multiple dwelling shall be designed for a live load of 40 pounds per square foot.
Live load means weight of

  A. floor joists, beams, and girders
  B. tenants only
  C. tenants and their furniture
  D. floor joists, beams, girders, tenants, and furniture

21. An anonymous complaint is made to the Department of Buildings.
This complaint should be

    A. ignored because it is not signed
    B. investigated because it may be valid
    C. filed to see if further complaints of a like nature are made
    D. ignored because only troublemakers make anonymous complaints

22. In order to make certain emergency repairs to an occupied multiple dwelling, a fire escape must be removed. The owner asks you, an inspector, for permission to do this.
You should

    A. grant the request, since the only way to make the repair is to remove the fire escape
    B. tell the owner to find another method of making the repair since a fire escape may not be removed
    C. refer the owner to your superiors, since you do not have the authority to grant the request
    D. grant the request only if fire extinguishers are provided to prevent danger of fire

23. The cellar ceiling of a converted multiple dwelling is to be fire-retarded by applying two layers of 1/2" plaster boards to the existing ceiling. The owner tells you that the existing lath is too weak to support the weight of the additional plaster boards.
You should

    A. insist that the plaster boards shall be applied on the existing ceiling
    B. tell the owner that the plaster boards will not be necessary since their application would be dangerous
    C. permit installation of only one layer of plaster boards in order to reduce the load on the lath
    D. require that the lath be strengthened first and then that the two layers of plaster boards be applied

24. A tenant has made a complaint that water leaking from a pipe in the apartment above has damaged the ceiling of the tenant's apartment. While the premises are being inspected, the tenant mentions other complaints to you. You should

    A. tell the tenant you are there to inspect the original complaint only
    B. listen courteously to the tenant, but discourage further complaints
    C. check each of the complaints to determine their validity
    D. place a violation on the landlord for all the complaints

25. The public halls of a multiple dwelling were painted two months ago. A tenant has filed a complaint stating that the walls are now peeling and are in a dirty, deteriorated condition. When investigating this complaint, you find that it is justified.
You should

    A. test the paint to find out why it peeled so rapidly
    B. notify the landlord to repaint the walls properly
    C. tell the tenant that since the walls were painted within three years, nothing further can be done
    D. refer the complaint to the legal department so that court action may be taken

26. A multiple dwelling is being erected with one wall on a lot line. On the adjoining lot is a two-family house. The owner of this house complaints that the new building is cutting off light and ventilation from the two-family house.
You should

   A. tell the small home owner that nothing can be done since the law permits such construction
   B. tell the small home owner that nothing can be done since two-family houses are not within your jurisdiction
   C. stop construction of the multiple dwelling since it is illegal to block ventilation of another house
   D. tell the small home owner to sue the city for the decrease in the value of his property

27. The approved plans for a converted multiple dwelling call for fireproofing the stair enclosure with metal lath and cement plaster. The contractor would like to substitute two layers of 1/2 inch plaster board since this has the same fire-resistive rating as the lath and plaster.
The inspector should

   A. permit this, since the fire ratings are the same
   B. deny this, since the structural strengths may not be the same
   C. permit this only if an amended plan showing the substitution is approved
   D. permit this only if the structural strengths and the fire-resistive ratings are the same

28. During a routine inspection of a multiple dwelling, an inspector discovers that a fire door has been blocked open.
The FIRST action of the inspector should be to

   A. order the owner or his representative to remove the blocking immediately
   B. notify the owner in writing that a violation of the law exists on the premises
   C. warn the tenants that a fire hazard exists
   D. remove the blocking himself

29. When writing a report of an investigation of a tenant's complaint, the item that you should consider LEAST important for inclusion in the report is the

   A. name of tenant   B. apartment number
   C. age of building   D. location of building

30. A tenant asks you about the procedures the Department of Buildings uses in processing a violation complaint.
You should

   A. refer the tenant to your superiors since they are the only ones permitted to give official information
   B. tell the tenant that such information is none of his business
   C. give the tenant the information in as concise a manner as possible
   D. explain completely and in detail all the ramifications of departmental procedure

31. In investigating the adequacy of the exits of a multiple dwelling, the LEAST important item to check is the

    A. location of exits
    B. width of stairs
    C. size of stair platforms
    D. number of treads and risers

32. In a 8-story fireproof multiple dwelling of skeleton steel construction, the one of the following members that would be LEAST likely to have a fire-resistive enclosure is a

    A. beam   B. column   C. joist   D. lintel

33. The one of the following that is LEAST related to the others is

    A. pile   B. footing   C. caisson   D. pilaster

34. A pit at the low point of a cellar floor is known as a(n)

    A. sump   B. well
    C. accumulator D. drain

35. The structure above the roof of a building that encloses a stairway is called a

    A. bulkhead   B. penthouse
    C. mezzanine D. stairwell

36. To prevent flying sparks, incinerator chimneys in multiple dwellings are frequently covered with

    A. cement copings B. draft hoods
    C. goosenecks   D. wire mesh

37. A valve used to prevent boiler explosions due to excessive pressure is a _____ valve.

    A. check   B. gate   C. relief   D. fuller

38. The one of the following that is acceptable according to the building code for a 3-hour fire partition is 6"

    A. solid brick
    B. solid stone concrete blocks
    C. solid cinder concrete blocks
    D. plain concrete

39. A fire tower is a

    A. means of egress from a building
    B. water tank on the roof of a building
    C. piece of Fire Department equipment
    D. draft space through which fire will spread

Questions 40-45.

DIRECTIONS: Questions 40 through 45, inclusive, refer to the sketch of an apartment building shown on the last page. All questions are to be answered on the basis of this sketch.

40. The dimension of the bedroom indicated by the letter Y is 40.____

    A. 9'1 5/16" B. 9'1 13/16"
    C. 9'2 3/16" D. 9'2 11/16"

41. Following is an abstract of the multiple dwelling law: 41.____
    1. Every living room (including bedrooms) shall contain at least 80 square feet of floor space.
    2. Every living room shall be at least eight feet in least horizontal dimension except that any number of bedrooms up to one-half the total number in any apartment containing three or more bedrooms may have a least horizontal dimension of seven feet or more.

    In order to increase the width of the hall, it is necessary to decrease the width of the bedroom indicated by the letter Y.
    The one of the following that is the smallest acceptable width of this room is

    A. 7'0" B. 7'6" C. 8'0" D. 8'6"

42. The columns shown are 42.____

    A. wood posts B. concrete filled pipes
    C. I beams D. built up channels

43. The letter indicating the partition that is MOST likely to be a bearing partition is 43.____

    A. M
    B. W
    C. X
    D. There are no bearing partitions

44. The exit door 44.____

    A. does not swing in the direction of egress
    B. is too large
    C. will block the stairs
    D. is not fireproof

45. The one of the following general notes that is MOST likely to appear in connection with this plan is: 45.____

    A. Masonry walls shall be braced horizontally at maximum intervals of twenty times the wall thickness
    B. Buttresses shall be bonded into the wall by masonry in the same manner as employed in the construction of the wall
    C. Masonry walls shall be anchored at maximum intervals of four feet, to each tier of joists bearing on such walls, by metal anchors
    D. Openings in the masonry wall shall be spanned by a lintel or arch of incombustible materia

8 (#1)

KEY (CORRECT ANSWERS)

1. C	11. D	21. B	31. D	41. D
2. C	12. B	22. C	32. D	42. B
3. A	13. B	23. D	33. D	43. D
4. D	14. C	24. C	34. A	44. C
5. B	15. A	25. B	35. A	45. C
6. C	16. C	26. A	36. D	
7. B	17. D	27. C	37. C	
8. A	18. A	28. A	38. C	
9. D	19. D	29. C	39. A	
10. B	20. C	30. C	40. D	

EXAMINATION SECTION
TEST 1

DIRECTIONS: Each question or incomplete statement is followed by several suggested answers or completions. Select the one that BEST answers the question or completes the statement. *PRINT THE LETTER OF THE CORRECT ANSWER IN THE SPACE AT THE RIGHT.*

1. The basis of differentiating between a *Class A* and a *Class B* multiple dwelling is

    A. the date when the building was erected
    B. the size of the building
    C. whether residents are permanent or transient
    D. the number of families living in the building

    1._____

2. The basis of differentiating between a *cellar* and a *basement* is

    A. whether or not there are windows
    B. the relationship of its height to curb level
    C. the ventilation available
    D. the number of exists provided

    2._____

3. The MINIMUM horizontal dimension permitted for a living room in an apartment house erected after 1929 is

    A. 8'0"   B. 8'6"   C. 9'0"   D. 9'6"

    3._____

4. It is proposed to build a garage for two cars for use by the tenants in a three-family dwelling. The garage will be on the same lot as the dwelling.
    Of the following, the statement that MOST completely gives the type or types of construction that would be permitted for the garage is _____ with concrete roof.

    A. frame or block walls with flat wood roof or block walls with wood peak roof, or block walls
    B. block walls with flat wood roof or block walls with wood peak roof or block walls
    C. block walls with wood peak roof or block walls
    D. block walls

    4._____

5. A restaurant is permitted in a hotel of non-fireproof construction providing that

    A. there are automatic sprinkler heads in the kitchen
    B. there are two means of egress from the kitchen
    C. the kitchen has windows opening to a required yard
    D. the walls of the kitchen have one hour fire rating

    5._____

6. The one of the following that is considered a *living room* is a

    A. bathroom   B. foyer
    C. public room   D. kitchen

    6._____

7. In certain types of occupancies, gas-fueled space heaters may be used instead of a central heating system. One of the requirements that MUST be met in order that space heaters be permitted in an apartment is that the

    7._____

27

2 (#1)

- A. building be of fireproof construction
- B. apartment must consist of two or more living rooms
- C. building is not a tenement
- D. apartment has two means of egress

8. Where a parapet wall is required, the MINIMUM height permitted is 8.___

   A. 3'0"   B. 3'6"   C. 4'0"   D. 4'6"

9. Ceilings over boilers in converted dwellings MUST be fire-retarded with 9.___

   - A. two layers of 3/8" sheet rock
   - B. wire lath and 3/4" cement mortar
   - C. 3/8" rock lath and 1/2" gypsum mortar
   - D. 3/8" sheet rock with #26 U.S. gage stamped metal

10. A fire alarm signal is required in all multiple dwellings which have the following type of occupancy: 10.___

    - A. tenement
    - B. hotel
    - C. converted dwelling
    - D. single room

11. The multiple dwelling law requires that every living room be ventilated by windows having an area of at least 10% of the floor surface of the room. Assume that a certain living room is 10'6" long by 9'6" wide. 11.___
    Of the following, the MINIMUM window size that would be acceptable is

    - A. 3'2" x 3'6"
    - B. 3'4" x 3'6"
    - C. 3'4" x 3'8"
    - D. 3'6" x 3'8"

12. The multiple dwelling law specifies the minimum area and height of living rooms. The PRINCIPAL reason for this is to 12.___

    - A. insure adequate light and air
    - B. make inspections easier
    - C. reduce possibility of serious fires
    - D. control the number of occupants

13. The one of the following that is considered a multiple dwelling when located in a building separate from other buildings is a 13.___

    - A. jail
    - B. monastery
    - C. nurses' residence
    - D. asylum

14. When any part of a building is to be fire-retarded, that part of the building MUST be protected by materials having a fire rating of at least _____ hour(s). 14.___

    A. 1   B. 2   C. 3   D. 4

15. A *fire damper* is necessary to 15.___

    - A. adjust the draft in a chimney
    - B. wet down combustible material in case of fire
    - C. prevent the passage of heat and smoke through an air duct
    - D. control the flame in an incinerator

Questions 16-18.

DIRECTIONS: Questions 16 through 18 must be answered in accordance with the following paragraph.

When constructed within a multiple dwelling, such storage space shall be equipped with a sprinkler system and also with a system of mechanical ventilation in no way connected with any other ventilating system. Such storage space shall have no opening into any other part of the dwelling except through a fireproof vestibule. Any such vestibule shall have a minimum superficial floor area of fifty square feet and its maximum area shall not exceed seventy-five square feet. It shall be enclosed with incombustible partitions having a fire-resistive rating of three hours. The floor and ceiling of such vestibule shall also be of incombustible material having a fire-resistive rating of at least three hours. There shall be two doors to provide access from the dwelling to the car storage space. Each such door shall have a fire-resistive rating of one and one-half hours and shall be provided with a device to prevent the opening of one door until the other door is entirely closed.

16. According to the above paragraph, the one of the following that is REQUIRED in order for cars to be permitted to be stored in a multiple dwelling is a(n)

    A. fireproof vestibule
    B. elevator from the garage
    C. approved heating system
    D. sprinkler system

17. According to the above paragraph, the one of the following materials that would NOT be acceptable for the walls of a vestibule connecting a garage to the dwelling portion of a building is

    A. 3" solid gypsum blocks
    B. 4" brick
    C. 4" hollow gypsum blocks, plastered both sides
    D. 6" solid cinder concrete blocks

18. According to the above paragraph, the one of the following that would be ACCEPTABLE for the width and length of a vestibule connecting a garage that is within a multiple dwelling to the dwelling portion of the building is

    A. 3'8" x 13'0"   B. 4'6" x 18'6"
    C. 4'9" x 14'6"   D. 4'3" x 19'3"

Questions 19-20.

DIRECTIONS: Questions 19 and 20 must be answered in accordance with the following paragraph.

It shall be unlawful to place, use, or to maintain in a condition intended, arranged or designed for use, any gas-fired cooking appliance, laundry stove, heating stove, range or water heater or combination of such appliances in any room or space used for living or sleeping in any new or existing multiple dwelling unless such room or space has a window opening to the outer air or such gas appliance is vented to the outer air. All automatically operated gas appliances shall be equipped with a device which shall shut off automatically the gas supply to the main burners when the pilot light in such appliance is extinguished. A gas range or the cooking portion of a gas appliance incorporating a room heater shall not be deemed an automatically operated gas appliance. However, burners in gas ovens and broilers which can be turned on and off or ignited by non-manual means shall be equipped with a device which shall shut off automatically the gas supply to those burners when the operation of such non-manual means fails.

19. According to the above paragraph, an automatic shut-off device is NOT required on a gas

    A. hot water heater
    B. laundry drier
    C. space heater
    D. range

20. According to the above paragraph, a gas-fired water heater is permitted

    A. only in kitchens
    B. only in bathrooms
    C. only in living rooms
    D. in any type of room

21. A tenant tells an inspector that the spring on the entrance door to his apartment is broken and the door remains open.
    Of the following, the BEST action for the inspector to take, after verifying the facts, is to

    A. tell the tenant to get the janitor to fix it
    B. tell the janitor to get it fixed
    C. tell the landlord to hire someone to fix it
    D. report it as a violation and tell the janitor to get it fixed

22. An owner of a two-family house tells you, an inspector, that he wants to convert his house to a three-family dwelling. He asks you for your advice as to the requirements that must be met for this change.
    You should

    A. inspect the building so that you can give him all the necessary information
    B. refer him to your supervisor for fuller advice
    C. tell him to consult a competent architect
    D. tell him you can't give him the information unless he gives you the plans of the building to check

23. An inspector receiving a complaint from a tenant should consider it as

    A. most likely the result of a quarrel with the landlord
    B. usually an exaggerated statement of the facts
    C. a matter which should be investigated
    D. something to be checked after all other work has been completed

24. In a dispute about a matter covered by the multiple dwelling law, an inspector should carefully AVOID

    A. taking the attitude that the landlord is always wrong
    B. sounding out both the landlord and the tenant when both sides disagree
    C. investigating the basis of the disagreement
    D. getting involved in the matter until both the landlord and the tenant agree on the facts

25. If an inspector does not clearly understand one of the provisions of the multiple dwelling law, he should

   A. interpret it as best he can
   B. get his superior to explain it to him
   C. avoid having to enforce this provision
   D. consider this provision unimportant

26. If a tenant continues to ask an inspector a great many questions, the inspector should

   A. tell the tenant not to ask so many questions because the inspector has too many other things to do
   B. pretend he does not hear the tenant unless the tenant persists
   C. tell the tenant that all questions should be referred to the main office
   D. answer the questions as briefly as he can without creating the impression he is trying to *brush off* the tenant

27. If an inspector is dissatisfied with his assignment, he should

   A. demand that he be re-assigned to another task
   B. slow down his work so that his superior knows he is dissatisfied
   C. continue doing his work as well as he can but request a reassignment at the earliest opportunity
   D. make sure his fellow inspectors know his feelings

28. The MAIN reason why an inspector should know the value of his work is that

   A. he will have more of an incentive to do a better job
   B. he can better explain his job to the public
   C. it will be easier for him to get a promotion
   D. he will be able to ignore minor inspections

29. A landlord has made an unjustified complaint about an inspector to the inspector's superiors.
   In future contacts with this landlord, the inspector should be

   A. cool and distant to avoid more trouble
   B. smiling and friendly to ease matters
   C. courteous and fair in enforcing the law
   D. strict so that the landlord knows he must comply with his orders

30. Assume that an inspector believes that one of the provisions of the multiple dwelling law is unfair.
   The inspector should

   A. refuse to enforce this provision because it is unfair
   B. enforce this provision because it does not matter whether the law is fair or not
   C. refuse to enforce this provision because it is impossible to make the public comply with this provision
   D. enforce the provision because it is the law

31. In wood frame construction, mortise and tenon joints may be illegal. The basis for determining whether or not such a joint is legal is

   A. type of wood
   B. size of members
   C. load carried by the members
   D. age of wood

32. Of the following terms, the one LEAST related to the others is

   A. scuttle   B. buttress   C. bulkhead   D. parapet

33. Of the following terms, the one LEAST related to the others is

   A. egress
   B. fire tower
   C. fire wall
   D. fire escape

34. A deformed bar would MOST likely be used in

   A. masonry work
   B. steel construction
   C. wood construction
   D. reinforced concrete construction

35. A party wall is a(n)

   A. wall serving two structures
   B. interior wall
   C. retaining wall
   D. wall without openings

36. Of the following types of walls, the one LEAST related to the others is

   A. faced   B. spandrel   C. apron   D. panel

37. A bar bending table would MOST likely be used in the following type of construction:

   A. steel
   B. reinforced concrete
   C. wood
   D. masonry

38. Of the following terms, the one which is LEAST related to the others is

   A. down-spout
   B. ground seat
   C. gutter
   D. leader

39. Of the following terms, the one which is LEAST related to the others is

   A. ball-peen
   B. doublecut flat
   C. file card
   D. rat tail

40. Of the following, the one which is LEAST related to the others is

   A. chase   B. footing   C. pier   D. pile

Questions 41-45.

DIRECTIONS: Questions 41 through 45 are to be answered in accordance with the floor plan of one floor of a converted dwelling shown on the last page of this test.

41. The depth of the linen closet, indicated by the letter S, is 41.____

    A. 1'4" B. 1'5" C. 1'6" D. 1'7"

42. The door that should have a fire rating is indicated by the letter 42.____

    A. G B. H C. J D. K

43. The walls of the building are of 43.____

    A. frame construction B. solid brick
    C. brick and block D. solid block

44. Of the following types of steel sections, the one that MOST closely resembles, in appearance, the steel beams used to support the floor joists is 44.____

    A. ⊔ B. ST C. L D. WF

45. The grade of lumber indicated for joists FORMERLY was called # 45.____

    A. 1 common B. 1 select C. 2 common D. 2 select

8 (#1)

FLOOR PLAN

KEY (CORRECT ANSWERS)

1. C	11. A	21. D	31. B	41. C
2. B	12. A	22. C	32. B	42. A
3. A	13. C	23. C	33. C	43. C
4. D	14. A	24. A	34. D	44. D
5. A	15. C	25. B	35. A	45. A
6. D	16. D	26. D	36. A	
7. B	17. B	27. C	37. B	
8. B	18. C	28. A	38. B	
9. B	19. D	29. C	39. A	
10. D	20. D	30. D	40. A	

EXAMINATION SECTION
TEST 1

DIRECTIONS: Each question or incomplete statement is followed by several suggested answers or completions. Select the one that BEST answers the question or completes the statement. *PRINT THE LETTER OF THE CORRECT ANSWER IN THE SPACE AT THE RIGHT.*

Questions 1-5.

DIRECTIONS: Questions 1 through 5 are to be answered on the basis of the following statement. Use ONLY the information contained in this statement in answering these questions.

No multiple dwelling shall be erected to a height in excess of one and one-half times the width of the widest street on which it faces, except that above the level of such height, for each one foot that the front wall of such dwelling sets back from the street line, three feet shall be added to the height limit of such dwelling, but such dwelling shall not exceed in maximum height three feet plus one and three-quarter times the width of the widest street on which it faces.

Any such dwelling facing a street more than one hundred feet in width shall be subject to the same height limitations as though such dwelling faced a street one hundred feet in width.

1. The MAXIMUM height of a multiple dwelling set back five feet from the street line and facing a 60 foot wide street is _____ feet.   1.____
   A. 60   B. 90   C. 105   D. 165

2. The MAXIMUM height of a multiple dwelling set back six feet from the street line and facing a 120 foot wide street is _____ feet.   2.____
   A. 198   B. 168   C. 120   D. 105

3. The MAXIMUM height of a multiple dwelling is   3.____
   A. 100 ft.   B. 150 ft.   C. 178 ft.   D. unlimited

4. The MAXIMUM height of a multiple dwelling set back 10 feet from the street line and facing a 110 foot wide street is _____ feet.   4.____
   A. 178   B. 180   C. 195   D. 205

5. The MAXIMUM height of a multiple dwelling set back eight feet from the street line and facing a 90 foot wide street is _____ feet.   5.____
   A. 135   B. 147   C. 178   D. 159

Questions 6-10.

DIRECTIONS: Questions 6 through 10 are to be answered on the basis of the following statement. Use ONLY the information contained in this statement in answering these questions.

2 (#1)

The number of persons accommodated on any story in a lodging house shall not be greater than the sum of the following components.
    a. 22 persons for each full multiple of 22 inches in the smallest clear width for each means of egress approved by the department, other than fire escapes.
    b. 20 persons for each lawful fire escape accessible from such story.

6. The MAXIMUM number of persons that may be accommodated on a story in a lodging house depends on the

    A. number of lawful fire escapes *only*
    B. number of approved means of egress *only*
    C. smallest clear width in each approved means of egress *only*
    D. number of lawful fire escapes and sum total of smallest clear widths in each approved means of egress

6.____

7. The MAXIMUM number of persons that may be accommodated on a story of a lodging house having one lawful fire escape and a sum total of 44 inches in the smallest clear widths of the two approved means of egress is

    A. 20   B. 22   C. 42   D. 64

7.____

8. The MAXIMUM number of persons that may be accommodated on a story of a lodging house having two lawful fire escapes and a sum total of 60 inches in the smallest clear width of the approved means of egress is

    A. 64   B. 84   C. 100   D. 106

8.____

9. The MAXIMUM number of persons that may be accommodated on a story of a lodging house having one lawful fire escape and a sum total of 33 inches in the smallest clear width of the approved means of egress is

    A. 42   B. 53   C. 64   D. 73

9.____

10. The MAXIMUM number of persons that may be accommodated on a story of a lodging house having two lawful fire escapes and two approved means of egress, with 40 inches and 44 inches in the smallest clear widths, respectively, is

    A. 84   B. 104   C. 106   D. 108

10.____

11. An employee of the Department of Housing and Buildings may take outside employment in private industry as a(n)

    A. architect   B. mason
    C. plumber   D. none of the above

11.____

12. The one of the following that is NOT a multiple dwelling is a

    A. college dormitory
    B. dwelling occupied by three families
    C. hospital
    D. lodging house

12.____

13. The one of the following that is a Class A multiple dwelling is a

    A. commercial building containing a janitor's apartment
    B. furnished room house

13.____

C. hotel
D. tenement

14. A dwelling occupied by one family with five transient roomers is a _____ dwelling.

    A. Class A multiple
    B. Class B multiple
    C. single family private
    D. two-family private

15. The one of the following that is deemed a living room by the multiple dwelling law is a

    A. bathroom
    B. bedroom
    C. dinette, 45 sq. ft. in area
    D. kitchenette, 45 sq. ft. in area

16. The MAXIMUM number of stories to which a new multiple dwelling may be erected without having a passenger elevator is

    A. 4   B. 5   C. 6   D. 7

17. In a new multiple dwelling, which of the following rooms are required to have windows?

    A. Bathroom
    B. Kitchen
    C. Water-closet compartment
    D. All of the above

18. New multiple dwellings three stories or more in height must have hot water supplied during

    A. the hours between 6 A.M. and Midnight *only*
    B. the hours between 8 A.M. and 8 P.M. *only*
    C. the hours between 6 A.M. and Noon and 6 P.M. and Midnight *only*
    D. all hours

19. A winding stair in a new multiple dwelling is

    A. not permitted under any circumstances
    B. permitted under all circumstances
    C. permitted only when the building is more than 6 stories high
    D. permitted only when the building is less than 6 stories high

20. All elevator shaft walls in new multiple dwellings MUST be

    A. at least 4 inches thick
    B. fireproof
    C. hollow
    D. made of gypsum plaster

21. The one of the following statements about new multiple dwellings that is NOT true is:

    A. Boiler rooms in multiple dwellings four stories or more in height must have fireproof doors
    B. Every open roof area must have a guard rail or parapet wall at least 3'6" high
    C. A new multiple dwelling may be placed on the same lot with a frame building
    D. A new multiple dwelling may be used for parking of passenger motor vehicles

22. A tenement within the meaning of the multiple dwelling law is a building erected BEFORE

   A. April 18, 1929
   B. April 6, 1948
   C. April 12, 1949
   D. March 25, 1952

23. Every entrance hall in a multiple dwelling must be provided with a light of AT LEAST _____ watts.

   A. 5   B. 10   C. 15   D. 40

24. From the entrance to the first stair, every entrance hall in a new multiple dwelling must be, in clear width, AT LEAST

   A. 3'8"   B. 4'   C. 6'   D. 8'

25. A basement in a new multiple dwelling exceeding seven stories in height MUST have AT LEAST one-half of its height _____ curb level and is _____ as a story.

   A. above; counted
   B. above; not counted
   C. below; counted
   D. below; not counted

26. The lower ends of mitred cross bridging should be nailed to the beams

   A. at the same time that the top ends are nailed
   B. before the rough flooring is placed
   C. after the plastering is complete
   D. after the flooring is placed

27. The maximum distance between lines of bridging should NOT exceed

   A. 10'0"   B. 8'0"   C. 6'6"   D. 4'6"

28. The building code states that it shall be unlawful to corbel walls less than twelve inches thick, except for fire-stopping.
   From this, it may be concluded that

   A. walls 12 inches or more in thickness shall not be corbelled
   B. if a wall is less than 12 inches thick, it is permissible to corbel provided some of the corbelling is used for fire-stopping
   C. fire-stopping shall not be considered to be corbelling
   D. corbelling and fire-stopping are the same

29. The building code states that curtain walls of solid masonry shall be at least eight inches thick for the uppermost thirteen feet and at least twelve inches thick for the next fifty-two feet or fraction thereof below and shall be increased four inches in thickness for each succeeding sixty feet or fraction thereof below.
   This means that the thickness of a solid masonry curtain wall 126 feet high should be AT LEAST

   A. 20 inches throughout its height
   B. 20 inches at the base
   C. 16 inches throughout its height
   D. 16 inches at the base

30. The term *curb cut* refers to

    A. openings in a curb
    B. tire cuts made while parking
    C. surveying marks chiseled in a curb
    D. rental for sidewalk stands

31. A bearing wall is a wall which

    A. carries its own weight *only*
    B. carries load other than its own weight
    C. bears on structural supports at each story
    D. is more than 12 feet high

32. A column is an _____ member.

    A. upright compression   B. inclined compression
    C. upright tension   D. inclined tension

33. A lintel could be broadly classified as a

    A. beam   B. column   C. footing   D. strut

34. A flat slab is MOST commonly used in _____ construction.

    A. sidewalk   B. roadway   C. conduit   D. building

35. Of the following, the member which would MOST likely be supported on a footing is the

    A. beam   B. girder   C. column   D. joist

36. A parapet wall would MOST likely support

    A. a coping   B. roof joists
    C. floor joists   D. partitions

37. Jack arches are used

    A. in ornamental iron work
    B. in fancy stairways
    C. when lintels are omitted
    D. in foundations

38. If green lumber is used for joists, shrinkage will have its MOST serious effect in _____ of joists.

    A. length   B. width   C. depth   D. weight

39. The phrase *concealed draft openings* is MOST likely to be used in connection with

    A. fireplaces   B. flues
    C. fire-stopping   D. automatic dampers

40. Of the following terms, the one which is LEAST related to the others is the

    A. jamb   B. strike plate
    C. latch bolt   D. pulley stile

Questions 41-45.

DIRECTIONS: Questions 41 through 45 are to be answered in accordance with the following sketch.

2ND. FL. PLAN

41. The one of the following statements that is CORRECT is: The building

　　A. is of fireproof construction
　　B. has masonry walls, with wood joists
　　C. is of wood frame construction
　　D. has timber posts and girders

41._____

42. The one of the following statements that is CORRECT is:

　　A. The stairway from the ground floor continues through the roof
　　B. There are two means of egress from the second floor of this building
　　C. The door on the second floor stair landing opens in the direction of egress
　　D. The entire stair is shown on this plan

42._____

43. The width of the hall is 43.____

    A. 10'3"   B. 10'5"   C. 10'7"   D. 10'9"

44. The lintels shown are 44.____

    A. angles
    B. a channel and an angle
    C. an I-beam
    D. precast concrete

45. The one of the following statements that is CORRECT is: The steel beam is 45.____

    A. supported by columns at the center and at the ends
    B. entirely supported by the walls
    C. supported on columns at the ends only
    D. supported at the center by a column and at the ends by the walls

KEY (CORRECT ANSWERS)

1. C	11. D	21. C	31. B	41. B
2. B	12. C	22. A	32. A	42. C
3. C	13. D	23. C	33. A	43. D
4. A	14. B	24. B	34. D	44. A
5. D	15. B	25. A	35. C	45. D
6. D	16. C	26. D	36. A	
7. D	17. D	27. B	37. C	
8. B	18. A	28. C	38. C	
9. A	19. A	29. B	39. C	
10. C	20. B	30. A	40. D	

EXAMINATION SECTION

DIRECTIONS: Each question or incomplete statement is followed by several suggested answers or completions. Select the one that BEST answers the question or or completes the statement. *PRINT THE LETTER OF THE CORRECT ANSWER IN THE SPACE AT THE RIGHT.*

1. A lintel is MOST CLOSELY associated with a
    A. wall opening
    B. floor opening
    C. roof opening
    D. fire escape

    1.____

2. An apron is MOST CLOSELY associated with a
    A. door
    B. window
    C. yard
    D. bulkhead

    2.____

3. In remodeling a multiple dwelling, brickwork has been removed from an interior steel column and replaced with 3/4" plaster. The MOST SERIOUS consequence of this alteration relates to
    A. strength
    B. corrosion
    C. fire
    D. accidental damage

    3.____

4. In multiple dwellings, hand-rails must be provided on each side of a stairway if the stairway exceeds CERTAIN
    A. height
    B. width
    C. steepness
    D. tread-riser ratio

    4.____

5. A rectangular court is 16'0" wide by 20'0" long. The length of a diagonal is, in feet, most nearly,
    A. 25.2
    B. 25.4
    C. 25.6
    D. 25.8

    5.____

6. If concrete weighs 4000 pounds per cubic yard, the weight of a slab of concrete 2'6" by 6'9" by 3'2" is, in pounds, most nearly,

    A. 7920
    B. 7830
    C. 7740
    D. 7650

    6.____

7. In the case of new construction, a certificate of occupancy is required for
    A. class A multiple dwellings
    B. class A and class B multiple dwellings
    C. all dwellings
    D. all buildings

    7.____

8. A sewer which carries BOTH sewage and storm water is known as a ____ sewer.
    A. sanitary
    B. combined
    C. separate
    D. storm

    8.____

9. A fire-restrictive rating of an assembly indicates that the assembly
    A. is incombustible
    B. is non-flammable
    C. can withstand a fire of given duration without serious failure
    D. prevents the passage of heat

    9.____

10. Major classifications of districts established by the Zoning Resolution do NOT Include _____ districts.
    A. Use   B. Height   C. Residence   D. Area

11. The distinction between a Business District and a Business-1 District relates to
    A. types of businesses
    B. size of businesses
    C. types of business signs
    D. area allowed for manufacturing

12. The MAXIMUM hight to which a multiple dwelling fronting on a 100-foot street may be erected in a class one and on-half district is
    A. 178 ft.   B. 175 ft.   C. 150 ft.   D. 125 ft.

13. As a senior supervisor of Housing, you are directed to interview several men whom the department is considering for provisional employment as a supervisor of Housing. During the course of your interview with one of these men, you learn that he has good building construction experience, owns his home outright in the City for the past four years, and even owns the patent rights on certain items now being used in building construction work. With respect to this man, you should recommend that he
    A. be employed for a trial period of 30 days
    B. be employed for a provisional period of 90 days
    C. should not be employed unless further questioning shows that he complies with the Residence Law
    D. should not be employed unless he divests himself of certain properties

14. Multiple dwellings of non-fireproof construction may NOT exceed
    A. 75 feet in height
    B. 6 stories in height unless provided with elevators
    C. 5 stories in height
    D. 60 feet in height

15. Construction in a non-fireproof multiple dwelling more than three stories high must be fireproof in all of the following locations EXCEPT
    A. first floor
    B. stairs
    C. elevator shaft below first floor
    D. roof

16. Flue or chimney connections for every apartment are MOST LIKELY to be required in
    A. tenements
    B. class A multiple dwellings
    C. class B multiple dwellings
    D. buildings used for single-room occupancy

17. In a 6-story multiple dwelling, the required access to the yard form a street may NOT be provided by a
    A. court
    B. fire proof passage
    C. fire-retarded passage
    D. direct passage 3'6" clear width by 7'0" high

18. The required area a function of the of windows in a living room is
    A. floor area
    B. room volume
    C. wall area
    D. number of occupants

19. A living room in a class A multiple dwelling is 8'0" wide by 9'6" long by 8'6" high. This room fails to meet requirements of the Multiple Dwelling Law with respect to
    A. height
    B. volume
    C. area
    D. least horizontal dimension

20. A tenant complains to an inspector that the interior lock on his dumbwaiter door is faulty and that the door is continually coming open. The inspector should, after verifying the facts,
    A. tell the tenant to notify the landlord
    B. notify the janitor and report a violation to the Department
    C. tell the tenant to fix it himself
    D. tell the janitor to fix this lock

21. Fire escapes constructed of material subject to rusting should be painted
    A. every year
    B. every two years
    C. whenever they become rusty
    D. twice a year

22. A building fronts on an unpaved street without curbs or sidewalk. The legal height of the building
    A. can not be established
    B. is established by the architect
    C. may be established from the equivalent curb level
    D. is established by the owner

23. The story heights of a class B multiple dwelling are as follows: cellar, 12 ft.; first floor, 20 ft.; second floor, 15 ft.; third through sixth floors, 12 ft. The story height of the building is
    A. 6
    B. 7
    C. 8
    D. 9

24. The distinction between "cellar" and "basement" is concerned with
    A. relative position with respect to curb elevation
    B. use
    C. height
    D. area

25. The distinction between fire-tower and fire-stair is based upon
    A. position with respect to building walls
    B. degree of fire-proofing
    C. height
    D. use of self-closing fireproof doors

26. Yards may NOT be omitted under any circumstances when a multiple dwelling occupies
    A. two or more entire blocks
    B. an interior lot
    C. an interior lot running through from street to street
    D. an entire block

27. A multiple dwelling is one which is occupied by at least
    A. 2 families   B. 3 families   C. 4 families   D. 5 familles

28. The distinction between class A and class B multiple dwellings relates to
    A. size   B. quality   C. fireproofing   D. residence

29. A portion of a multiple dwelling which is considered to be an apartment contains
    A. more than one room
    B. a kitchen
    C. a bathroom
    D. a water-closet compartment

30. Living rooms include
    A. water-closet compartments
    B. bathrooms
    C. kitchens
    D. foyers

31. Of the following, the one which is NOT considered to be an alteration is
    A. replacing wainscoting with plaster
    B. moving a building from one lot to another
    C. replacing bearing wall to make one large room from two small ones
    D. increasing the height of a building without increasing the number of stories

32. A trimmer arch is used in connection with a
    A. fireplace   B. window   C. closet door   D. stairway

33. A sidewalk shed
    A. is never permitted
    B. is used-when demolishing buildings
    C. is allowed in front of public buildings
    D. must have an open roof

Questions 34-39.
Questions 34 through 39 refer to the two columns below. Each item in Column 1 is associated with an item in Column 2. Place the letter of the item in Column 2 after the number of the item in Column 1 with which it is most closely associated. Items in Column 2 may be used more than once or not at all.

Column 1	Column 2	
34. Scratch coat	A. Welding	34._____
35. Flashing	B. Bricklaying	35._____
36. Louvre	C. Plumbing	36._____
37. Bond	D. Plastering	37._____
38. Soil stack	E. Roofing	38._____
39. Shoring	F. Flooring	39._____
	G. Excavating	
	H. Ventilatin	

40. Of the following terms, the one which LEAST relates to the other is 40._____
    A. soffit   B. newel   C. nosing   D. trimmer

41. Of the following terms, the one which LEAST relates to the others is 41._____
    A. muntin   B. stop-bead   C. jamb   D. sill

42. Fire-stopping is synonymous with 42._____
    A. fireproofing
    B. fire-retarding
    C. fire-treated
    D. none of the foregoing

43. A two-story building 32'0" by 60'0" is erected on a lot 75'0" by 110'0". The floor area 43._____
    ratio is, most nearly,
    A. 0.46   B. 0.42   C. 0.38   D. 0.34

44. A portion of a multiple dwelling, other than an apartment or suite of rooms, separated as 44._____
    a unit from the rest of the building by fireproof construction, is known as a
    A. section   B. unit   C. separate   D. wing

45. Records maintained by the Department for each building in the City should 45._____
    include all of the following EXCEPT
    A. number of persons living in each apartment
    B. diagram of building
    C. date of erection
    D. deaths occurring in building each year

46. Hospitals are required to make a weekly report to the Department of cases of
    sickness received in such hospital. This report does NOT state
    A. patient's name
    B. patient's address
    C. patient's sickness
    D. whether patient is an adult or child

47. The Police Department is required to make a weekly report to the Department of arrests. The report does NOT contain
    A. name
    B. address
    C. offense
    D. disposition of case

48. Of the following City Departments, the one which must be furnished information by the Department is
    A. Hospitals
    B. Welfare
    C. Public Works
    D. Tax

49. In a new multiple dwelling, gas meters may be located in
    A. boiler rooms
    B. stair halls
    C. public halls above the cellar
    D. none of the foregoing

50. A required sink may be placed in a
    A. bathroom containing a water-closet
    B. water-closet compartment
    C. public hall
    D. none of the foregoing

(KEY (CORRECT ANSWERS)

1. A	11. C	21. C	31. A	41. C
2. B	12. A	22. C	32. A	42. D
3. C	13. D	23. C	33. B	43. A
4. B	14. A	24. A	34. D	44. A
5. C	15. D	25. A	35. E	45. A
6. A	16. A	26. B	36. H	46. A
7. D	17. C	27. B	37. B	47. D
8. B	18. A	28. D	38. C	48. D
9. C	19. C	29. C	39. G	49. D
10. C	20. B	30. C	40. D	50. D

EXAMINATION SECTION
TEST 1

DIRECTIONS: Each question or incomplete statement is followed by several suggested answers or completions. Select the one that BEST answers the question or completes the statement. *PRINT THE LETTER OF THE CORRECT ANSWER IN THE SPACE AT THE RIGHT.*

Questions 1-5.

DIRECTIONS: For Questions 1 through 5, inclusive, Column I lists frequently used construction terms. Column II lists some of the building trades. For each item listed in Column I, enter in the appropriate space at the right the capital letter in front of the trade listed in Column II that is MOST closely associated with the item. Each trade may be used more than once or not at all.

COLUMN I	COLUMN II	
1. Bed	A. Plumbing	1.____
2. Wiping	B. Plastering	2.____
3. Brown	C. Carpentry	3.____
4. Key	D. Masonry	4.____
5. Bridging	E. Painting	5.____
	F. Steelwork	
	G. Roofing	

6. A *cricket* would be found 6.____

   A. on a roof
   B. at a structural steel connection
   C. supporting reinforcing steel
   D. over a window

7. *Cutting in* is done when 7.____

   A. trimming a stud to size
   B. fitting a bat in a brick wall
   C. painting in tight corners
   D. trimming tallow for a wiped joint

8. *Corbeling* results in 8.____

   A. strengthening a concrete column
   B. waterproofing a foundation wall
   C. anchoring a steel girder to a bearing wall
   D. increasing the thickness of a brick wall

9. Solder used for copper gutters is MOST frequently

   A. 30-70   B. 40-60   C. 50-50   D. 60-40

10. A jack rafter runs from

    A. plate to ridge
    B. hip to ridge
    C. plate to hip
    D. plate to plate

11. The one of the following items that is LEAST related to the others is

    A. sill   B. joist   C. sole   D. newel

12. A *fire cut* is made on

    A. timber posts
    B. rafters
    C. floor joists
    D. lathing

13. The one of the following items that is LEAST related to the others is

    A. joist hanger
    B. pintle
    C. bridle iron
    D. stirrup

14. The PROPER order of nailing sub-flooring and bridging is

    A. top of bridging, bottom of bridging, sub-flooring
    B. bottom of bridging, sub-flooring, top of bridging
    C. top of bridging, sub-flooring, bottom of bridging
    D. bottom of bridging, top of bridging, sub-flooring

15. Sleepers would be found in

    A. walls   B. doors   C. footings   D. floors

16. The one of the following woods that is MOST commonly used for finish flooring is

    A. hemlock   B. cypress   C. larch   D. oak

17. Spacing of studs in a stud partition is MOST frequently _____ " o.c.

    A. 12   B. 14   C. 16   D. 18

18. A hollow masonry wall should be used in preference to a solid masonry wall when the characteristic MOST desired is

    A. insulation
    B. strength
    C. beauty
    D. durability

19. The arrangement of headers and stretchers in brickwork is known as the

    A. bond   B. stringer   C. lacing   D. stile

20. Of the following, the reason that is LEAST likely to justify pointing brickwork is that pointing _____ the wall.

    A. improves the appearance of
    B. helps prevent cracking of
    C. increases the useful life of
    D. helps waterproof

21. The purpose of flashing is to 21.____

    A. keep water out   B. speed the set of mortar
    C. anchor a cornice   D. cover exposed joists

22. The one of the following classes of wall that would LEAST likely be the outside wall of a building is a 22.____

    A. spandrel   B. fire   C. curtain   D. parapet

23. Lime is added to mortar USUALLY to 23.____

    A. increase the strength of the mortar
    B. make the mortar water resistant
    C. make it easier to apply the mortar
    D. improve the appearance of the mortar joint

24. Efflorescence on the face of a brick wall is BEST removed by scrubbing with a solution of 24.____

    A. muriatic acid   B. sodium silicate
    C. oxalic acid   D. calcium oxide

25. The one of the following that is NOT a defect in painting is 25.____

    A. chalking   B. checking
    C. alligatoring D. waning

26. The one of the following ingredients of a paint that would be called the *vehicle* is 26.____

    A. white lead   B. turpentine
    C. linseed oil   D. pigment

27. The one of the following that is used as a rust preventative in the prime coat for painting steel is 27.____

    A. aluminum   B. red lead
    C. titanium dioxide D. carbon black

28. *Boxing*, with reference to paint, means 28.____

    A. thinning   B. mixing   C. spreading   D. drying

29. When painting new wood, filling of nail holes and cracks with putty should be done 29.____

    A. 24 hours before priming
    B. immediately before priming
    C. after priming and before the second coat
    D. after the second coat and before the finish coat

30. The one of the following that is the size of a reinforcing rod MOST commonly used in reinforced concrete construction is 30.____

    A. 1 3/4" ϕ B. 18 gauge   C. #9   D. 2 ST3

31. Honeycombing in concrete is USUALLY caused by 31.____

    A. too plastic a mix   B. high fall of concrete
    C. mixing too long   D. inadequate vibration

32. A concrete mix is indicated as 1:2:3 1/2 mix. The number *2* refers to the proportion by volume of

    A. water B. cement C. gravel D. sand

33. Specifications for concrete mixes frequently call for the use of dry sand. The reason for this is that the additional water in wet sand will

    A. make it more difficult to place the concrete
    B. decrease the strength of the concrete
    C. cause the sand and stone to segregate
    D. increase the cost of waterproofing

34. Curing of concrete serves PRIMARILY to

    A. prevent freezing of the concrete
    B. permit early removal of forms
    C. delay setting of the concrete
    D. prevent evaporation of moisture

35. The MAIN reason that forms for concrete work are oiled is to

    A. *permit* easy removal of forms
    B. *prevent* rust marks on the concrete
    C. *prevent* bleeding of water
    D. *permit* easier vibration of the concrete

36. The one of the following terms that is LEAST related to the others is

    A. 5-ply   B. mastic
    C. vapor barrier   D. flashing

37. Before quicklime can be used for plaster, it must be

    A. slaked B. burned C. floated D. glazed

38. When a hard plaster is required, as in halls, the one of the following that would MOST likely be used is

    A. lime   B. Keene's cement
    C. stucco   D. marbling

39. To give plaster a hard finish, hydrated lime is mixed with

    A. white cement   B. linseed oil putty
    C. white lead   D. plaster of paris

40. The purpose of a ground in plaster work is to

    A. provide a key for the plaster
    B. help the plasterer make an even wall
    C. prevent the plasterer's scaffold from slipping
    D. hold the loose plaster before it is placed

41. When a lightweight plaster is required, the one of the following fine aggregates that is MOST likely to be used is

    A. cinders
    B. sand
    C. talc
    D. vermiculite

42. Of the following fireproofing materials, the one which would be MOST frequently used to fireproof steel columns in a fireproof building is

    A. sheet rock
    B. vermiculite plaster
    C. brick
    D. rock lath

43. The one of the following items that is LEAST related to the others is

    A. rock wool
    B. wall board
    C. sheet rock
    D. rock lath

44. The first layer of plaster placed in a 3-coat plaster job is called the _____ coat.

    A. brown   B. scratch   C. hard   D. white

45. The one of the following symbols that represents a steel section which is MOST similar in appearance to a W section is

    A. U   B. L   C. I   D. Z

46. A plate used to connect two steel angles in a roof truss is known as a(n)

    A. angle iron
    B. gusset plate
    C. bearing plate
    D. tie bar

47. Steel beams are COMMONLY anchored to brick walls by

    A. government anchors
    B. tie rods
    C. eye bars
    D. anchor bolts

48. Rivet holes are lined up with a

    A. set screw
    B. ginnywink
    C. drift pin
    D. trivet

49. A sewer that carries BOTH storm water and sewage is called a _____ sewer.

    A. sanitary   B. flush   C. combined   D. mixed

50. A fresh air inlet for a house drainage system would be connected to the system

    A. just ahead of the house trap
    B. at each horizontal branch line
    C. at the top of the stack through the roof
    D. at the trap of each water closet

KEY (CORRECT ANSWERS)

1. D	11. D	21. A	31. D	41. D
2. A	12. C	22. B	32. D	42. B
3. B	13. B	23. C	33. B	43. A
4. B	14. C	24. A	34. D	44. B
5. C	15. D	25. D	35. A	45. C
6. A	16. D	26. C	36. C	46. B
7. C	17. C	27. B	37. A	47. A
8. D	18. A	28. B	38. B	48. C
9. C	19. A	29. C	39. D	49. C
10. C	20. B	30. C	40. B	50. A

TEST 2

DIRECTIONS: Each question or incomplete statement is followed by several suggested answers or completions. Select the one that BEST answers the question or completes the statement. *PRINT THE LETTER OF THE CORRECT ANSWER IN THE SPACE AT THE RIGHT.*

Questions 1-5.

DIRECTIONS: Column I consists of a list of trades, and Column II lists tools used in those trades. In the space at the right, opposite the number of the trade in Column I, write the letter preceding the tool of the trade in Column II.

COLUMN I		COLUMN II	
1. Carpenter	A.	Mop	1.____
2. Plumber	B.	Hawk	2.____
3. Plasterer	C.	Miter box	3.____
4. Bricklayer	D.	Shave-hook	4.____
5. Roofer	E.	Jointing tool	5.____

Questions 6-7.

DIRECTIONS: Questions 6 and 7 refer to the mortar joints shown below.

6. The mortar joint MOST frequently used on common brickwork is 6.____
   A. 1   B. 2   C. 3   D. 4

7. The mortar joint which would NOT usually be made unless an outside scaffold was used is 7.____
   A. 1   B. 2   C. 3   D. 4

8. A rectangular yard is 50'0" long by 8'6" wide. 8.____
   The area of the yard is, in square feet,
   A. 420.0   B. 422.5   C. 425.0   D. 427.5

9. A rectangular court is 23'0" long by 9'6" wide. The length of the diagonal is MOST NEARLY

   A. 24'8"   B. 24'10"   C. 25'2"   D. 25'6"

10. Concrete weighs 150 pounds per cubic foot.
    A slab of concrete 6'0" long by 3'6" wide by 1'4" thick weighs MOST NEARLY _____ pounds.

    A. 4150   B. 4200   C. 4250   D. 4300

11. A building 32'0" by 65'0" occupies a lot 60'0" by 110'0". The ratio of building area to lot area is MOST NEARLY

    A. 0.32   B. 0.33   C. 0.34   D. 0.35

12. When painting wood, puttying of nail holes and cracks is done

    A. before any painting is started
    B. after the priming coat is applied
    C. after the finish coat is applied
    D. at any stage in the painting

13. The process of pouring paint from one container to another in order to mix it is known as

    A. bleeding   B. boxing   C. cutting   D. stirring

14. Paint is *thinned* with

    A. linseed oil   B. turpentine
    C. varnish   D. gasoline

15. A wood screw which can be tightened by a wrench is known as a _____ screw.

    A. lag   B. Philips   C. carriage   D. monkey

16. To permit easy removal of forms from concrete, the inside surfaces of the forms are often coated with

    A. paint   B. oil   C. water   D. asphalt

17. Sixteen pieces of 2 x 4 lumber, each 10'6" long, contain a total of _____ FBM.

    A. 110   B. 111   C. 112   D. 113

18. The consistency of concrete is measured with a

    A. Vicat needle   B. slump cone
    C. hook gage   D. bourdon gage

19. End-matched lumber would MOST likely be used for

    A. sheathing   B. roofing   C. flooring   D. siding

20. A post or shore is to be placed midway between columns to support the formwork for a reinforced concrete girder. The post should be cut

    A. short, so that wedging is required
    B. to exact length

C. long, so that it will have to be driven into place
D. in two pieces, to permit jackknifing into place

21. Batter boards are set by a

    A. mason   B. plumber   C. roofer   D. surveyor

22. Of the following terms, all of which refer to tools, the one which is LEAST related to the others is

    A. back   B. box-end   C. cross-cut   D. rip

23. Of the following tools, the one which is LEAST like the others is

    A. brace and bit   B. draw-knife
    C. plans   D. spoke-shave

24. When wood splits easily, it is advisable to drill a hole for each nail. The hole for the nail should be _____ the nail.

    A. larger in diameter than
    B. smaller in diameter than
    C. exactly the same diameter as
    D. less than one-quarter the length of

25. The length of a 10-penny nail, in inches, is

    A. $2\frac{1}{2}$ B. 3   C. $3\frac{1}{2}$ D. 4

26. The decimal equivalent of 31/64 of an inch is MOST NEARLY

    A. 0.45   B. 0.46   C. 0.47   D. 0.48

27. Of the following, the one which is BEST classified as an abrasive is

    A. a saw   B. a chisel   C. graphite   D. sandpaper

28. Of the following construction materials, the one which would MOST likely be stored directly on the ground is

    A. brick   B. cement   C. steel   D. wood

29. The strength of brick walls is based upon the type of mortar used. The relative strength of the various types of mortar, in descending order, is

    A. cement, lime, cement-lime
    B. lime, cement-lime, cement
    C. cement-lime, cement, lime
    D. cement, cement-lime, lime

30. Coating reinforcing rods with oil before placing them in the forms is

    A. *good* practice, because it prevents rusting
    B. *poor* practice, because it makes the rods difficult to handle
    C. *good* practice if the forms are oiled
    D. *poor* practice, because it destroys the bond between the concrete and the rods

31. If the mixing plant should break down after one-half the concrete has been mixed for a floor, the BEST thing to do would be to

   A. take the concrete out of the forms and throw it away
   B. spread the available concrete evenly over the floor area
   C. block off one-half of the floor area and place the available concrete in the blocked-off area
   D. keep mixing the concrete in the forms with shovels until the plant is repaired

32. Splicing of reinforcing bars is accomplished by

   A. using wire ties
   B. underlapping the bars
   C. hooking the bars
   D. using metal clips

33. A sanitary sewer carries

   A. storm water only
   B. sewage only
   C. sewage and storm water
   D. the discharge from a sewage plant

34. A neat line

   A. is the result of good workmanship
   B. is used in concrete construction only
   C. defines an outer limit of a structure
   D. defines an outer limit of excavation for a structure

35. Continued trowelling of a cement-finish floor for a building is

   A. *good* practice, because it provides a smooth floor
   B. *poor* practice, because it produces a slippery floor
   C. *poor* practice, because it brings the fines to the surface
   D. *good* practice, because it insures proper mixing of the cement finish

36. In reinforced concrete form work, a beveled chamfer strip is used to

   A. reinforce the outside of the forms
   B. reinforce the inside of the forms
   C. seal leaks in the forms
   D. do none of the foregoing

37. Cracks in lumber due to contraction along annual rings are known as

   A. checks
   B. wanes
   C. pitch pockets
   D. dry rot

38. Honeycombing is MOST likely to occur in construction involving

   A. steel   B. concrete   C. wood   D. masonry

39. Floor beams are sometimes crowned to

   A. provide arch action
   B. eliminate deflection
   C. strengthen the floor
   D. provide a more nearly level floor than would be provided by straight beams

40. In brickwork, a rowlock course consists of

    A. headers
    B. stretchers
    C. bricks laid on edge
    D. bricks laid so that the longest dimension is vertical

41. The term *bond,* as used in bricklaying, refers to

    A. structure only
    B. pattern only
    C. structure and pattern
    D. color and finish of individual bricks

42. Concrete is a mixture of cement,

    A. fine aggregate, coarse aggregate, and water
    B. sand, and water
    C. stone, and water
    D. sand, and stone

43. Consistency, when used in connection with concrete, refers to the

    A. seven-day strength
    B. twenty-eight day strength
    C. initial set before forms are removed
    D. plasticity of freshly mixed concrete

44. Brick may be used for the facing material in both faced walls and veneered walls. The distinction between the two types of walls relates to

    A. bonding or lack of bonding between facing and backing
    B. type of material in facing and backing
    C. relative thickness of facing and backing
    D. the type of mortar used

45. A plaster *key* is NOT formed on _____ lath.

    A. wood   B. metal
    C. expanded metal D. gypsum

46. Of the following, the BEST tool to use to make a hole in a coping stone is a

    A. star drill   B. coping saw
    C. pneumatic grinder D. diamond wheel dresser

47. Roughing refers to work performed by a

    A. carpenter   B. bricklayer
    C. plumber   D. roofer

48. A post supporting a handrail is known as a

    A. tread   B. riser   C. newel   D. bevel

49. The live load on a floor is 40 pounds per square foot. The floor joists are on a 14'0" span and are spaced 2'6" on centers.
   The maximum live load carried by a joist, in pounds, is MOST NEARLY

   A. 700   B. 933   C. 1167   D. 1400

50. Of the following terms, the one LEAST related to the others is

   A. ground
   B. purlin
   C. rafter
   D. ridge board

KEY (CORRECT ANSWERS)

1. C	11. A	21. D	31. C	41. C
2. D	12. B	22. B	32. A	42. A
3. B	13. B	23. A	33. B	43. D
4. E	14. B	24. B	34. C	44. A
5. A	15. A	25. B	35. C	45. D
6. C	16. B	26. D	36. D	46. A
7. A	17. C	27. D	37. A	47. C
8. C	18. B	28. A	38. B	48. C
9. B	19. C	29. D	39. D	49. D
10. B	20. A	30. D	40. C	50. A

EXAMINATION SECTION
TEST 1

DIRECTIONS: Each question or incomplete statement is followed by several suggested answers or completions. Select the one that BEST answers the question or completes the statement. *PRINT THE LETTER OF THE CORRECT ANSWER IN THE SPACE AT THE RIGHT.*

1. Assume that a two story building measures 21'6" x 53'7". It is in a district that calls for an open space ratio of .80. The required open space on this lot must be *most nearly* square feet.   1._____

    A. 922   B. 1152   C. 1843   D. 2880

2. Assume that the elevation at the back of a lot is 127.36 ft. and the elevation at the front of the same lot is 125.49 ft.
The difference in elevation between front and back of the lot is *most nearly*   2._____

    A. 1'10 1/8"   B. 1'10 1/4"   C. 1'10 3/8"   D. 1'10 1/2"

3. The sketch below represents the lowest story of a new building. In order for this story to be considered a basement, the elevation of the first floor must be AT LEAST   3._____

    A. 131.09   B. 131.14   C. 131.19   D. 131.24

4. The MOST important requirement of a good report is that it should be   4._____

    A. properly addressed
    B. clear and concise
    C. verbose
    D. spelled correctly

5. Of the following, in determining whether a violation should be referred for court action, the MOST important item that should be considered is   5._____

    A. the amount of available time you have to process the case
    B. the availability of the inspector
    C. whether or not the owner has indicated a desire to cooperate with the department
    D. whether or not the case is important enough to warrant court action

6. In the Zoning Resolution, the size of required side yards would be found in the chapters on

    A. Use Groups
    B. Bulk Regulations
    C. Area Districts
    D. District Boundaries

7. According to the Zoning Resolution, the one of the following that is NOT considered part of the floor area of a building is a(n)

    A. basement
    B. stairwell at floor level
    C. penthouse
    D. attached garage on 1st floor

8. The one of the following that is permitted by the Zoning Resolution as a home occupation is

    A. veterinary medicine
    B. real estate broker
    C. teaching of music
    D. public relations agency

9. For the purpose of determining the number of rooms in a dwelling unit, the Zoning Resolution adds an arbitrary number to the number of *living rooms*.
    Where there are six or less living rooms, this arbitrary number is

    A. 1/2   B. 1   C. 1 1/2   D. 2

10. Assuming the following signs are all 10 square feet in area, the one that is NOT subject to the provisions of the Zoning Resolution is one indicating

    A. a freight entrance to a building
    B. a fund drive for a civic organization
    C. vacancies in an apartment building
    D. a parking area at the rear of a structure

11. On a plan, the symbol ⎯⎯⎯ represents

    A. earth
    B. wood
    C. metal lath
    D. marble

12. On a plan, the symbol represents

    A. cinder
    B. brick
    C. plywood
    D. rock lath and plaster

13. On a plan, the symbol represents

    A. glass
    B. asphalt shingles
    C. concrete
    D. porcelain enamel

14. A corbel is a form of

    A. cricket B. crown molding
    C. cantilever D. curtain wall

15. In balloon type framing, the second floor joists rest on a

    A. sole plate B. ribband
    C. header D. sill

16. Condensation of moisture in inadequately ventilated attics or roof spaces is usually GREATEST in

    A. summer B. autumn C. winter D. spring

17. Of the following combinations of tread and riser, the one that would be acceptable for required stairs in either a new office building or a multiple dwelling is

    A. 9 1/4", 7 1/2" B. 9 1/2", 7 1/4"
    C. 9 1/2", 7 3/4" D. 10", 8"

18. A meeting rail is a common part of a

    A. door frame B. window sash
    C. stairwell D. bulkhead

19. If doors in an old building do not close, it is MOST probably an indication that the

    A. frames have shrunk
    B. building has settled
    C. hinges were not set properly
    D. wood used for the doors are of inferior grade

20. Cracks in concrete are not necessarily caused by settlement of a structure. Sometimes they are caused by

    A. shrinkage B. curing
    C. hydration D. over-troweling

KEY (CORRECT ANSWERS)

1. C
2. D
3. A
4. B
5. C

6. B
7. D
8. C
9. C
10. B

11. A
12. B
13. A
14. C
15. B

16. C
17. C
18. B
19. B
20. A

TEST 2

DIRECTIONS: Each question or incomplete statement is followed by several suggested answers or completions. Select the one that BEST answers the question or completes the statement. *PRINT THE LETTER OF THE CORRECT ANSWER IN THE SPACE AT THE RIGHT.*

1. Required exit doors from a room must open in the direction of egress when the room is occupied by more than _____ persons. 1.____

   A. 15   B. 25   C. 35   D. 50

2. A window in a masonry wall on a lot line 2.____

   A. is not permitted
   B. must have a fire resistive rating of 3/4 hour
   C. must have a fire resistive rating of 1 hour
   D. must have a fire resistive rating of 1 1/2 hours

3. Air entrained concrete is required in all cases for 3.____

   A. garage floors   B. footings
   C. grade beams   D. columns

4. A parapet wall or railing would be required on new non-residential structures where the height of the structure is greater than (give lowest height specified by law) _____ feet. 4.____

   A. 15   B. 19   C. 22   D. 25

5. Of the following statements, the one that is CORRECT is that wood joists may 5.____

   A. not be supported on a fire wall
   B. be supported on a fire wall only if fireproofed wall is used
   C. be supported on a fire wall only if they are separated from each other by at least 4 inches of solid masonry
   D. be supported on a fire wall only if they are separated from each other by at least 12 inches of solid masonry

6. A foundation wall below grade may be of hollow block only if the building 6.____

   A. is a residence
   B. is no more than one story high
   C. is of frame construction
   D. has no cellar or basement

7. The Building Code specifies that lintels are required to be fire-proofed when the opening is more than _____ feet. 7.____

   A. 3   B. 4   C. 5   D. 6

8. In a 12-inch brick wall, the MAXIMUM permitted depth of a chase is 8.____

   A. none   B. 4"   C. 6"   D. 8"

9. Wood joists should clear flues and chimneys by at least 9.____

   A. 1"   B. 2"   C. 3"   D. 4"

10. Fire retarding or enclosure in shafts of all vent ducts are required when they

   A. go through more than one floor
   B. are used for intake as well as exhaust
   C. are more than 144 square inches in area
   D. are in rooms subdivided with wood partitions

11. Assume a builder is unable to complete the pour for a continuous concrete floor slab. The slab is supported by beams and girders.
    The construction joint should be made at a point

   A. over a beam
   B. one quarter of the span length from the beam
   C. one third of the span length from the beam
   D. midway between beams

12. Under required stairs in a Class 3 building,

   A. it is unlawful to locate a closet
   B. a closet is permitted provided that the stringers are fire retarded
   C. a closet is permitted provided that the closet is completely lined with incombustible material
   D. a closet is permitted provided that fireproof wood is used to frame out the closet

13. In New York City, the exit provisions of the State Labor Law apply

   A. only to factories
   B. to factories and warehouses
   C. to factories, warehouses, and restaurants
   D. to all types of uses

14. A Class 3 building, two stories high, may have required stairs enclosed with stud partitions fire retarded with gypsum boards unless the building is used for a

   A. factory
   B. storage warehouse
   C. bowling alley
   D. department store

15. The one of the following rooms in a *place of assembly* that is required to be sprinklered is a

   A. performer's dressing room
   B. kitchen
   C. service pantry
   D. waiting room

16. Of the following, the FIRST operation in the demolition of a building is the

   A. shoring of the adjoining buildings
   B. erection of railings around stairwells
   C. removal of windows
   D. venting of the roof

17. As used in the Building Code, *consistency* of concrete refers to

   A. composition
   B. water-cement ratio
   C. relative plasticity
   D. proportion of aggregates

18. One condition that is required for a building to be considered a *Special Occupancy Structure* is that the building is used for 18.____

    A. a theater
    B. a church
    C. a restaurant
    D. motor vehicle repairs

19. A wire glass vision panel on a door opening into a fire tower is 19.____

    A. not permitted
    B. permitted if the panel has a fire rating of 3/4 hour
    C. permitted if the panel has a fire rating of 3/4 hour and is less than 100 square inches in area
    D. permitted if the panel has a fire rating of 3/4 hour, is less than 100 square inches in area, and is glazed with two thicknesses of wire glass with an air space between

20. One of the requirements that must be met before untreated wood can be used as a subdividing partition in a Class 1 building is that the partition 20.____

    A. be no more than 8 feet high
    B. enclose an area less than 200 square feet in size
    C. enclose office space only
    D. be made of a single thickness of wood

KEY (CORRECT ANSWERS)

1.	D	11.	D
2.	B	12.	C
3.	A	13.	A
4.	C	14.	C
5.	C	15.	A
6.	D	16.	C
7.	B	17.	C
8.	B	18.	A
9.	D	19.	A
10.	A	20.	D

TEST 3

DIRECTIONS: Each question or incomplete statement is followed by several suggested answers or completions. Select the one that BEST answers the question or completes the statement. *PRINT THE LETTER OF THE CORRECT ANSWER IN THE SPACE AT THE RIGHT.*

1. There are two criteria required for determining whether a multiple dwelling shall be classified as a *converted dwelling*.
   The FIRST is the number of families originally occupying the dwelling, and the second is the

   A. conjunctive uses
   B. date of erection of the building
   C. classification, whether Class A or B
   D. number of families now occupying the dwelling

   1.___

2. According to the Multiple Dwelling Law, a *dinette* is NOT considered a living room if its area is _____ sq. ft. or less.

   A. 50   B. 55   C. 59   D. 64

   2.___

3. Where a building faces only one street, the curb level used for measuring the height of the building is the

   A. lowest curb level in front of the building
   B. highest curb level in front of the building
   C. level of the curb at the center of the front of the building
   D. average of the levels of the lowest and highest curb level in front of the building

   3.___

4. According to the Multiple Dwelling Code, one of the living rooms in each apartment of a newly created multiple dwelling shall have a MINIMUM floor area of _____ square feet.

   A. 59   B. 110   C. 150   D. 175

   4.___

5. It is proposed to alter an old law tenement so as to increase the number of apartments. Of the following, the one that MOST completely gives the requirements to be met before the alteration can be approved is: Each new apartment must be provided a

   A. water closet
   B. water closet and a wash basin
   C. water closet, a wash basin, and a bath or shower
   D. water closet, a wash basin, a bath or shower, and centrally supplied heat

   5.___

6. Gas fueled space heaters may be permitted in lieu of centrally supplied heat.
   One of the following conditions required before the use of space heaters can be permitted is that

   A. each apartment has no more than two living rooms
   B. the building is a Class A multiple dwelling
   C. all apartments are used for single room occupancy
   D. D, the gas line supplying the heater be connected directly to the main so that the tenant cannot control the flow of gas

   6.___

7. An incinerator is required in all multiple

   A. dwellings
   B. dwellings four or more stories in height
   C. dwellings four or more stories in height and occupied by more than twelve families
   D. dwellings four or more stories in height occupied by more than twelve families and erected after October 1, 1951

8. Tests of required sprinkler systems in a single room occupancy building must be made

   A. monthly
   B. quarterly
   C. semi-annually
   D. annually

9. An additional apartment may be created on the first floor of a Class A frame converted dwelling provided that no more than two families will occupy this floor and

   A. the entrance hall is sprinklered
   B. the building is brick veneered
   C. there is no basement occupancy
   D. all stairs are enclosed in one hour fire partitions

10. The MAIN feature differentiating a *five tower* from a *fire stair* is the

    A. fire rating of the enclosure walls
    B. use to which the fire tower is put
    C. method of entering the fire tower from the building
    D. height of the fire tower

11. A new elevator shaft is to be built into a non-fireproof multiple dwelling. Of the following materials, the one that has the lowest fire resistance that would be acceptable for the enclosure walls of this shaft is

    A. 3" solid gypsum block
    B. 2" x 4" studs with 5/8" fire code 60 each side
    C. steel studs, wire mesh and 3/4" P.C. plaster
    D. 4" hollow concrete blocks, plastered both sides

12. Of the following statements, the one that is MOST complete and accurate is that a frame extension 70 sq. ft. in area added to a frame multiple dwelling is

    A. not permitted
    B. permitted only if the walls of the extension are brick filled
    C. permitted only if the walls of the extension are brick filled and the extension is to be used solely for bathrooms
    D. permitted only if the walls of the extension are brick filled, the extension is to be used solely for bathrooms and the walls are at least 3 ft. from the side lot lines

13. Assume it is proposed to extend a business use in a non-fireproof multiple dwelling by erecting an extension at the rear of the building. The roof the extension is required to be fireproof

    A. in all cases
    B. when the business use requires a combustible occupancy permit
    C. when there are fire escapes above the extension
    D. if the business use is a factory

14. In a Class A dwelling, two water closets may   14.____

    A. be placed in one compartment only in old law tenements
    B. be placed in one compartment in either old law or new law tenements
    C. be placed in one compartment in all types of apartment houses
    D. not be placed in one compartment

15. According to the Multiple Dwelling Law, a janitor is NOT required when the maximum   15.____
    number of families occupying the dwelling is

    A. 6   B. 9   C. 12   D. 15

16. The first floor above the lowest cellar in a non-fireproof multiple dwelling does NOT have   16.____
    to be fireproof if

    A. the cellar is used only for incombustible storage
    B. there are two means of egress from the cellar
    C. the building is no more than three stories in height
    D. the dwelling is occupied by no more than nine families

17. In a converted multiple dwelling, ventilation of a room on the top story may be obtained   17.____
    by

    A. a skylight
    B. a duct with a wind blown hood
    C. a duct with an electrically operated fan
    D. by a window only and no other method is acceptable

18. *It* is proposed to build a closet under the stairs leading to the second floor in a non-fire-   18.____
    proof *new law* tenement. This is

    A. not permitted
    B. permitted only if the entire closet is built of non-combustible materials
    C. permitted only if the closet is used for non-combustible storage
    D. permitted if the closet is built of fire-retarded partitions and the soffit of the stairs is
       also fire-retarded

19. For multiple dwellings erected after April 18, 1929, a ladder from a fire escape to a roof is   19.____
    NOT required when

    A. the building is three stories or less in height
    B. the roof is built of incombustible material
    C. the fire escape is on the front of the building
    D. there is no safe access from the roof to another building

20. It is proposed to convert a Class B multiple dwelling used for summer resort occupancy   20.____
    to year-round Class B use. This conversion is

    A. illegal
    B. legal provided the exits comply with the requirements for Class B use
    C. legal provided the exits and toilet facilities comply with the requirements for Class
       B use
    D. legal provided the exits, toilet facilities, and ventilation requirements comply with
       the requirements for Class B use

KEY (CORRECT ANSWERS)

1. B
2. B
3. C
4. C
5. D

6. B
7. D
8. D
9. B
10. C

11. A
12. A
13. C
14. A
15. C

16. C
17. A
18. A
19. C
20. A

READING COMPREHENSION
UNDERSTANDING AND INTERPRETING WRITTEN MATERIAL
EXAMINATION SECTION
TEST 1

DIRECTIONS: Each question or incomplete statement is followed by several suggested answers or completions. Select the one that BEST answers the question or completes the statement. *PRINT THE LETTER OF THE CORRECT ANSWER IN THE SPACE AT THE RIGHT.*

Questions 1-3.

DIRECTIONS: Questions 1 through 3, inclusive, are to be answered in accordance with the following paragraph.

All cement work contracts, more or less, in setting. The contraction in concrete walls and other structures causes fine cracks to develop at regular intervals. The tendency to contract increases in direct proportion to the quantity of cement in the concrete. A rich mixture will contract more than a lean mixture. A concrete wall which has been made of a very lean mixture and which has been built by filling only about one foot in depth of concrete in the form each day will frequently require close inspection to reveal the cracks.

1. According to the above paragraph,

    A. shrinkage seldom occurs in concrete
    B. shrinkage occurs only in certain types of concrete
    C. by placing concrete at regular intervals, shrinkage may be avoided
    D. it is impossible to prevent shrinkage

1.____

2. According to the above paragraph, the one of the factors which reduces shrinkage in concrete is the

    A. volume of concrete in wall
    B. height of each day's pour
    C. length of wall
    D. length and height of wall

2.____

3. According to the above paragraph, a rich mixture

    A. pours the easiest
    B. shows the largest amount of cracks
    C. is low in cement content
    D. need not be inspected since cracks are few

3.____

Questions 4-6.

DIRECTIONS: Questions 4 through 6, inclusive, are to be answered SOLELY on the basis of the following paragraph.

It is best to avoid surface water on freshly poured concrete in the first place. However, when there is a very small amount present, the recommended procedure is to allow it to evaporate before finishing. If there is considerable water, it is removed with a broom, belt, float, or by other convenient means. It is never good practice to sprinkle dry cement, or a mixture of cement and fine aggregate, on concrete to take up surface water. Such fine materials form a layer on the surface that is likely to dust or hair check when the concrete hardens.

4. The MAIN subject of the above passage is

   A. surface cracking of concrete
   B. evaporation of water from freshly poured concrete
   C. removing surface water from concrete
   D. final adjustments of ingredients in the concrete mix

5. According to the above passage, the sprinkling of dry cement on the surface of a concrete mix would MOST LIKELY

   A. prevent the mix from setting
   B. cause discoloration on the surface of the concrete
   C. cause the coarse aggregate to settle out too quickly
   D. cause powdering and small cracks on the surface of the concrete

6. According to the above passage, the thing to do when considerable surface water is present on the freshly poured concrete is to

   A. dump the concrete back into the mixer and drain the water
   B. allow the water to evaporate before finishing
   C. remove the water with a broom, belt, or float
   D. add more fine aggregate but not cement

Questions 7-9.

DIRECTIONS: Questions 7 through 9, inclusive, are to be answered ONLY in accordance with the information given in the paragraph below.

Before placing the concrete, check that the forms are rigid and well braced and place the concrete within 45 minutes after mixing it. Fill the forms to the top with the wearing-course concrete. Level off the surfaces with a strieboard. When the concrete becomes stiff but still workable (in a few hours), finish the surface with a wood float. This fills the hollows and compacts the concrete and produces a smooth but gritty finish. For a non-gritty and smoother surface (but one that is more slippery when wet), follow up with a steel trowel after the water sheen from the wood-troweling starts to disappear. If you wish, slant the tread forward a fraction of an inch so that it will shed rain water.

7. Slanting the tread a fraction of an inch gives a surface that will

   A. have added strength
   B. not be slippery when wet
   C. shed rain water
   D. not have hollows

8. In addition to giving a smooth but gritty finish, the use of a wood float will tend to   8.____

   A. give a finish that is slippery when wet
   B. compact the concrete
   C. give a better wearing course
   D. provide hollows to retain rain water

9. Which one of the following statements is most nearly correct?   9.____

   A. Having checked the forms, one may place the concrete immediately after mixing same.
   B. One must wait at least 15 minutes after mixing the concrete before it may be placed in the forms.
   C. A gritty compact finish and one which is more slippery when wet will result with the use of a wood float.
   D. A steel trowel used promptly after a wood float will tend to give a non-gritty smooth finish.

Questions 10-11.

DIRECTIONS: Questions 10 and 11 are to be answered SOLELY on the basis of information contained in the following paragraph.

Tools and plastering methods have changed very little over the years. Most of the changes are mere improvements of the basic tools. The tools formerly made by hand are now machine-made and are *rigidly* constructed of light, but strong, materials in contrast to the clumsy constructions of the early types. The power-driven mixers and hoisting equipment used on large plastering jobs today produce better mortars and lighten the tasks involved.

10. According to the above paragraph, present day tools used for plastering   10.____

    A. have made plastering much more complicated than it used to be
    B. are heavier than the old-fashioned tools they replaced
    C. produce poorer results but speed up the job
    D. are lighter and stronger than the hand-made tools of the past

11. As used in the above paragraph, the word *rigidly* means MOST NEARLY   11.____

    A. feeble   B. weakly   C. firmly   D. flexibly

Questions 12-18.

DIRECTIONS: Questions 12 through 18 are to be answered in accordance with the following paragraphs.

SURFACE RENEWING OVERLAYS

A surface renewing overlay should consist of material which can be constructed in very thin layers. The material must fill surface voids and provide an impervious skid-resistant surface. It must also be sufficiently resistant to traffic abrasion to provide an economical service life.

Materials meeting these requirements are:
- a. Asphalt concrete having small particle size
- b. Hot sand asphalts
- c. Surface seal coats

Fine-graded asphalt concrete or hot sand asphalt can be constructed in layers as thin as one-half inch and fulfill all requirements for surface renewing overlays. They are recommended for thin resurfacing of pavements having high traffic volumes, as their service lives are relatively long when constructed properly. They can be used for minor leveling, they are quiet riding, and their appearance is exceptionally pleasing. Seal coats or slurry seals may fulfill surface requirements for low traffic pavements.

12. A surface renewing overlay must fill surface voids, provide an impervious skid-resistant surface, and

    A. be resistant to traffic abrasion
    B. have small particle size
    C. be exceptionally pleasing in appearance
    D. be constructed in half-inch layers

13. An *impervious skid-resistant surface* means a surface that is

    A. rough to the touch and fixed firmly in place
    B. waterproof and provides good gripping for tires
    C. not damaged by skidding vehicles
    D. smooth to the touch and quiet riding

14. The number of types of materials that can be constructed in very thin layers and are also suitable for surface renewing overlays is

    A. 1   B. 2   C. 3   D. 4

15. The SMALLEST thickness of asphalt concrete or hot sand asphalt that can fulfill all requirements for surface renewing overlays is _____ inch(es).

    A. ¼   B. ½   C. 1   D. 2

16. The materials that are recommended for thin resurfacing of pavements having high traffic volumes are

    A. those that have relatively long service lives
    B. asphalt concretes with maximum particle size
    C. surface seal coats
    D. slurry seals with voids

17. Fine-graded asphalt concrete and hot sand asphalt are quiet riding and are also

    A. recommended for low traffic pavements
    B. used as slurry seal coats
    C. suitable for major leveling
    D. exceptionally pleasing in appearance

18. The materials that may fulfill surface requirements for low traffic pavements are 18.____

    A. fine-graded asphalt concretes
    B. hot sand asphalts
    C. seal coats or slurry seals
    D. those that can be used for minor leveling

Questions 19-25.

DIRECTIONS: Questions 19 through 25 are to be answered SOLELY on the basis of the paragraphs below.

OPEN-END WRENCHES

Solid, non-adjustable wrenches with openings in one or both ends are called open-end wrenches. Wrenches with small openings are usually shorter than wrenches with large openings. This proportions the lever advantage of the wrench to the bolt or stud and helps prevent wrench breakage or damage to the bolt or stud.

Open-end wrenches may have their jaws parallel to the handle or at angles anywhere up to 90 degrees. The average angle is 15 degrees. This angular displacement variation permits selection of a wrench suited for places where there is room to make only a part of a complete turn of a nut or bolt. Handles are usually straight, but may be curved. Those with curved handles are called S-wrenches. Other open-end wrenches may have offset handles. This allows the head to reach nut or bolt heads that are sunk below the surface.

There are a few basic rules that you should keep in mind when using wrenches. They are:

    I. ALWAYS use a wrench that fits the nut properly. Otherwise, the wrench may slip, or the nut may be damaged.
    II. Keep wrenches clean and free from oil. Otherwise, they may slip, resulting in possible serious injury to you or damage to the work.
    III. Do NOT increase the leverage of a wrench by placing a pipe over the handle. Increased leverage may damage the wrench or the work.

19. Open-end wrenches 19.____

    A. are adjustable
    B. are solid
    C. always have openings at both ends
    D. are always S-shaped

20. Wrench proportions are such that wrenches with _____ openings have _____ handles. 20.____

    A. larger; shorter B. smaller; longer
    C. larger; longer   D. smaller; thicker

21. The average angle between the jaws and the handle of a wrench is _____ degrees. 21.____

    A. 0   B. 15   C. 22   D. 90

22. Offset handles are intended for use MAINLY with 22.___

    A. offset nuts
    B. bolts having fine threads
    C. nuts sunk below the surface
    D. bolts that permit limited swing

23. The wrench which is selected should fit the nut properly because this 23.___

    A. prevents distorting the wrench
    B. insures use of all wrench sizes
    C. avoids damaging the nut
    D. overstresses the bolt

24. Oil on wrenches is 24.___

    A. *good* because it prevents rust
    B. *good* because it permits easier turning
    C. *bad* because the wrench may slip off the nut
    D. *bad* because the oil may spoil the work

25. Extending the handle of a wrench by slipping a piece of pipe over it is considered 25.___

    A. *good* because it insures a tight nut
    B. *good* because less effort is needed to loosen a nut
    C. *bad* because the wrench may be damaged
    D. *bad* because the amount of tightening can not be controlled

---

KEY (CORRECT ANSWERS)

1.	D	11.	C
2.	B	12.	A
3.	B	13.	B
4.	C	14.	C
5.	D	15.	B
6.	C	16.	A
7.	C	17.	D
8.	B	18.	C
9.	A	19.	B
10.	D	20.	C

21.	B
22.	C
23.	C
24.	C
25.	C

TEST 2

DIRECTIONS: Each question or incomplete statement is followed by several suggested answers or completions. Select the one that BEST answers the question or completes the statement. *PRINT THE LETTER OF THE CORRECT ANSWER IN THE SPACE AT THE RIGHT.*

Questions 1-3.

DIRECTIONS: Questions 1 through 3 are to be answered SOLELY on the basis of the following passage.

A utility plan is a floor plan which shows the layout of a heating, electrical, plumbing, or other utility system. Utility plans are used primarily by the persons reponsible for the utilities, but they are important to the craftsman as well. Most utility installations require the leaving of openings in walls, floors, and roofs for the admission or installation of utility features. The craftsman who is, for example, pouring a concrete foundation wall must study the utility plans to determine the number, sizes, and locations of the openings he must leave for piping, electric lines, and the like.

1. The one of the following items of information which is LEAST likely to be provided by a utility plan is the

   A. location of the joists and frame members around stairwells
   B. location of the hot water supply and return piping
   C. location of light fixtures
   D. number of openings in the floor for radiators

1.____

2. According to the passage, the persons who will *most likely* have the GREATEST need for the information included in a utility plan of a building are those who

   A. maintain and repair the heating system
   B. clean the premises
   C. paint housing exteriors
   D. advertise property for sale

2.____

3. According to the passage, a repair crew member should find it MOST helpful to consult a utility plan when information is needed about the

   A. thickness of all doors in the structure
   B. number of electrical outlets located throughout the structure
   C. dimensions of each window in the structure
   D. length of a roof rafter

3.____

Questions 4-9.

DIRECTIONS: Questions 4 through 9 are to be answered SOLELY on the basis of the following passage.

The basic hand-operated hoisting device is the tackle or purchase, consisting of a line called a fall, reeved through one or more blocks. To hoist a load of given size, you must set up a rig with a safe working load equal to or in excess of the load to be hoisted. In order to do this, you must be able to calculate the safe working load of a single part of line of given size, the safe working load of a given purchase which contains a line of given size, and the minimum size of hooks or shackles which you must use in a given type of purchase to hoist a given load. You must also be able to calculate the thrust which a given load will exert on a gin pole or a set of shears inclined at a given angle, the safe working load which a spar of a given size used as a gin pole or as one of a set of shears will sustain, and the stress which a given load will set up in the back guy of a gin pole or in the back guy of a set of shears inclined at a given angle.

4. The above passage refers to the lifting of loads by means of

   A. erected scaffolds
   B. manual rigging devices
   C. power-driven equipment
   D. conveyor belts

5. It can be concluded from the above passage that a set of shears serves to

   A. absorb the force and stress of the working load
   B. operate the tackle
   C. contain the working load
   D. compute the safe working load

6. According to the above passage, a spar can be used for a

   A. back guy   B. block   C. fall   D. gin pole

7. According to the above passage, the rule that a user of hand-operated tackle MUST follow is to make sure that the safe working load is AT LEAST

   A. equal to the weight of the given load
   B. twice the combined weight of the block and falls
   C. one-half the weight of the given load
   D. twice the weight of the given load

8. According to the above passage, the two parts that make up a tackle are

   A. back guys and gin poles
   B. blocks and falls
   C. rigs and shears
   D. spars and shackles

9. According to the above passage, in order to determine whether it is safe to hoist a particular load, you MUST

   A. use the maximum size hooks
   B. time the speed to bring a given load to a desired place
   C. calculate the forces exerted on various types of rigs
   D. repeatedly lift and lower various loads

Questions 10-15.

DIRECTIONS: Questions 10 through 15 are to be answered SOLELY on the basis of the following set of instructions.

PATCHING SIMPLE CRACKS IN A BUILT-UP ROOF

If there is a visible crack in built-up roofing, the repair is simple and straightforward:

1. With a brush, clean all loose gravel and dust out of the crack, and clean three or four inches around all sides of it.
2. With a trowel or putty knife, fill the crack with asphalt cement and then spread a layer of asphalt cement about 1/8 inch thick over the cleaned area.
3. Place a strip of roofing felt big enough to cover the crack into the wet cement and press it down firmly.
4. Spread a second layer of cement over the strip of felt and well past its edges.
5. Brush gravel back over the patch.

10. According to the above passage, in order to patch simple cracks in a built-up roof, it is necessary to use a

    A. putty knife and a drill
    B. knife and pliers
    C. tack hammer and a punch
    D. brush and a trowel

11. According to the above passage, the size of the area that should be clear of loose gravel and dust before the asphalt cement is first applied should

    A. be the exact size of the crack itself
    B. extend three or four inches on all sides of the crack
    C. be 1/8 inch greater than the size of the crack itself
    D. extend the length of the roofing strip

12. According to the above passage, loose gravel and dust in the crack should be removed with a

    A. brush   B. felt pad   C. trowel   D. dust mop

13. Assume that both layers of asphalt cement needed to patch the crack are of the same thickness.
    The total thickness of asphalt cement used in the patch should be MOST NEARLY _____ inch.

    A. 1/2   B. 1/3   C. 1/4   D. 1/8

14. According to the instructions in the above passage, how large should the strip of roofing felt be cut?

    A. Three of four inches square
    B. Smaller than the crack and small enough to be surrounded by cement on all sides of the strip
    C. Exactly the same size and shape of the area covered by the wet cement
    D. Large enough to completely cover the crack

15. The final or finishing action to be taken in patching a simple crack in a built-up roof is to

    A. clean out the inside of the crack
    B. spread a layer of asphalt a second time
    C. cover the crack with roofing felt
    D. cover the patch of roofing felt and cement with gravel

Questions 16-17.

DIRECTIONS: Questions 16 and 17 are to be answered SOLELY on the basis of the information given in the following paragraph.

Supplies are to be ordered from the stockroom once a week. The standard requisition form, Form SP21, is to be used for ordering all supplies. The form is prepared in triplicate, one white original and two green copies. The white and one green copy are sent to the stockroom, and the remaining green copy is to be kept by the orderer until the supplies are received.

16. According to the above paragraph, there is a limit on the 16.___
    A. amount of supplies that may be ordered
    B. day on which supplies may be ordered
    C. different kinds of supplies that may be ordered
    D. number of times supplies may be ordered in one year

17. According to the above paragraph, when the standard requisition form for supplies is prepared, 17.___
    A. a total of four requisition blanks is used
    B. a white form is the original
    C. each copy is printed in two colors
    D. one copy is kept by the stock clerk

Questions 18-21.

DIRECTION: Questions 18 through 21 are to be answered SOLELY on the basis of the following passage.

The Oil Pollution Act for U. S. waters defines an *oily mixture* as 100 parts or more of oil in one million parts of mixture. This mixture is not allowed to be discharged into the prohibited zone. The prohibited zone may, in special cases, be extended 100 miles out to sea but, in general, remains at 50 miles offshore. The United States Coast Guard must be contacted to report all *oily mixture* spills. The Federal Water Pollution Control Act provides for a fine of $10,000 for failure to notify the United States Coast Guard. An employer may take action against an employee if the employee causes an *oily mixture* spill. The law holds your employer responsible for either cleaning up or paying for the removal of the oil spillage.

18. According to the Oil Pollution Act, an *oily mixture* is defined as one in which there are 18.___
    _____ parts or more of oil in _____ parts of mixture.
    A. 50; 10,000   B. 100; 10,000
    C. 100; 1,000,000   D. 10,000; 1,000,000

19. Failure to notify the proper authorities of an *oily mixture* spill is punishable by a fine. Such 19.___
    fine is provided for by the
    A. United States Coast Guard
    B. Federal Water Pollution Control Act
    C. Oil Pollution Act
    D. United States Department of Environmental Protection

20. According to the law, the one responsible for the removal of an *oily mixture* spilled into U.S. waters is the

    A. employer
    B. employee
    C. U.S. Coast Guard
    D. U.S. Pollution Control Board

21. The *prohibited zone,* in general, is the body of water

    A. within 50 miles offshore
    B. beyond 100 miles offshore
    C. within 10,000 yards of the coastline
    D. beyond 10,000 yards from the coastline

Questions 22-25.

DIRECTIONS: Questions 22 through 25 are to be answered SOLELY on the basis of the following paragraph.

Synthetic detergents are materials produced from petroleum products or from animal or vegetable oils and fats. One of their advantages is the fact that they can be made to meet a particular cleaning problem by altering the foaming, wetting, and emulsifying properties of a cleaner. They are added to commonly used cleaning materials such as solvents, water, and alkalies to improve their cleaning performance. The adequate wetting of the surface to be cleaned is paramount in good cleaning performance. Because of the relatively high surface tension of water, it has poor wetting ability, unless its surface tension is decreased by addition of a detergent or soap. This allows water to flow into crevices and around small particles of soil, thus loosening them.

22. According to the above paragraph, synthetic detergents are made from all of the following EXCEPT

    A. petroleum products   B. vegetable oils
    C. surface tension oils   D. animal fats

23. According to the above paragraph, water's poor wetting ability is related to

    A. its low surface tension
    B. its high surface tension
    C. its vegetable oil content
    D. the amount of dirt on the surface to be cleaned

24. According to the above paragraph, synthetic detergents are added to all of the following EXCEPT

    A. alkalines   B. water   C. acids   D. solvents

25. According to the above paragraph, altering a property of a cleaner can give an advantage in meeting a certain cleaning problem.
The one of the following that is NOT a property altered by synthetic detergents is the cleaner's

    A. flow ability
    B. foaming property
    C. emulsifying property
    D. wetting ability

25.___

KEY (CORRECT ANSWERS)

1.	A	11.	B
2.	A	12.	A
3.	B	13.	C
4.	B	14.	D
5.	A	15.	D
6.	D	16.	D
7.	A	17.	B
8.	B	18.	C
9.	C	19.	B
10.	D	20.	A

21. A
22. C
23. B
24. C
25. A

REPORT WRITING

EXAMINATION SECTION

TEST 1

DIRECTIONS: Each question or incomplete statement is followed by several suggested answers or completions. Select the one that BEST answers the question or completes the statement. *PRINT THE LETTER OF THE CORRECT ANSWER IN THE SPACE AT THE RIGHT.*

1. Following are six steps that should be taken in the course of report preparation:
   I. Outlining the material for presentation in the report
   II. Analyzing and interpreting the facts
   III. Analyzing the problem
   IV. Reaching conclusions
   V. Writing, revising, and rewriting the final copy
   VI. Collecting data

   According to the principles of good report writing, the CORRECT order in which these steps should be taken is:
   A. VI, III, II, I, IV, V
   B. III, VI, II, IV, I, V
   C. III, VI, II, I, IV, V
   D. VI, II, III, IV, I, V

   1.____

2. Following are three statements concerning written reports:
   I. Clarity is generally more essential in oral reports than in written reports.
   II. Short sentences composed of simple words are generally preferred to complex sentences and difficult words.
   III. Abbreviations may be used whenever they are customary and will not distract the attention of the reader.

   Which of the following choices correctly classifies the above statements in to those which are valid and those which are not valid?
   A. I and II are valid, but III is not valid
   B. I is valid, but II and III are not valid.
   C. II and III are valid, but I is not valid.
   D. III is valid, but I and II are not valid.

   2.____

3. In order to produce a report written in a style that is both understandable and effective, an investigator should apply the principles of unit, coherence, and emphasis.
   The one of the following which is the BEST example of the principle of coherence is
   A. interlinking sentences so that thoughts flow smoothly
   B. having each sentence express a single idea to facilitate comprehension
   C. arranging important points in prominent positions so they are not overlooked
   D. developing the main idea fully to insure complete consideration

   3.____

4. Assume that a supervisor is preparing a report recommending that a standard work procedure be changed.
Of the following, the MOST important information that he should include in this report is
   A. a complete description of the present procedure
   B. the details and advantages of the recommended procedure
   C. the type and amount of retraining needed
   D. the percentage of men who favor the change

4._____

5. When you include in your report on an inspection some information which you have obtained from other individuals, it is MOST important that
   A. this information have no bearing on the work these other people are performing
   B. you do not report as fact the opinions of other individuals
   C. you keep the source of the information confidential
   D. you do not tell the other individuals that their statements will be included in your report

5._____

6. Before turning in a report of an investigator of an accident, you discover some additional information you did not know about when you wrote the report. Whether or not you re-write your report to include this additional information should depend MAINLY on the
   A. source of this additional information
   B. established policy covering the subject matter of the report
   C. length of the report and the time it would take you to re-write it
   D. bearing this additional information will have on the conclusions in the report

6._____

7. The MOST desirable *first* step in the planning of a written report is to
   A. ascertain what necessary information is readily available in the files
   B. outline the methods you will employ to get the necessary information
   C. determine the objectives and uses of the report
   D. estimate the time and cost required to complete the report

7._____

8. In writing a report, the practice of taking up the least important points and the most important points last is a
   A. *good* technique since the final points made in a report will make the greatest impression on the reader
   B. *good* technique since the material is presented in a more logical manner and will lead directly to the conclusions
   C. *poor* technique since the reader's time is wasted by having to review irrelevant information before finishing the report
   D. *poor* technique since it may cause the reader to lose interest in the report and arrive at incorrect conclusions about the report

8._____

9. Which one of the following serves as the BEST guideline for you to follow for effective written reports?
Keep sentences
   A. short and limit sentences to one thought
   B. short and use as many thoughts as possible
   C. long and limit sentences to one thought
   D. long and use as many thoughts as possible

9.____

10. One method by which a supervisor might prepare written reports to management is to begin with the conclusions, results, or summary, and to follow this with the supporting data.
The BEST reason why management may *prefer* this form of report is that
   A. management lacks the specific training to understand the data
   B. the data completely supports the conclusions
   C. time is saved by getting to the conclusions of the report first
   D. the data contains all the information that is required for making the conclusions

10.____

11. When making written reports, it is MOST important that they be
   A. well-worded   B. accurate as to the facts
   C. brief   D. submitted immediately

11.____

12. Of the following, the MOST important reason for a supervisor to prepare good written reports is that
   A. a supervisor is rated on the quality of his reports
   B. decisions are often made on the basis of the reports
   C. such reports take less time for superiors to review
   D. such reports demonstrate efficiency of department operations

12.____

13. Of the following, the BEST test of a good report is whether it
   A. provides the information needed
   B. shows the good sense of the writer
   C. is prepared according to a proper format
   D. is grammatical and neat

13.____

14. When a supervisor writes a report, he can BEST show that he has a understanding of the subject of the report by
   A. including necessary facts and omitting nonessential details
   B. using statistical data
   C. giving his conclusions but not the data on which they are based
   D. using a technical vocabulary

14.____

15. Suppose you and another supervisor on the same level are assigned to work together on a report. You disagree strongly with one of the recommendations the other supervisor wants to include in the report but you cannot change his views.

15.____

Of the following, it would be BEST that
- A. you refuse to accept responsibility for the report
- B. you ask that someone else be assigned to this project to replace you
- C. each of you state his own ideas about this recommendation in the report
- D. you give in to the other supervisor's opinion for the sake of harmony

16. Standardized forms are often provided for submitting reports. 16._____
Of the following, the MOST important advantage of using standardized forms for reports is that
    - A. they take less time to prepare than individually written reports
    - B. the person making the report can omit information he considers unimportant
    - C. the responsibility for preparing these reports can be turned over to subordinates
    - D. necessary information is less likely to be omitted

17. A report which may BEST be classed as a *periodic* report is one which 17._____
    - A. requires the same type of information at regular intervals
    - B. contains detailed information which is to be retained in permanent records
    - C. is prepared whenever a special situation occurs
    - D. lists information in graphic form

18. In the writing of reports or letters, the ideas presented in a paragraph are usually of unequal importance and require varying degrees of emphasis. 18._____
All of the following are methods of placing extra stress on an idea EXCEPT
    - A. repeating it in a number of forms
    - B. placing it in the middle of the paragraph
    - C. placing it either at the beginning or at the end of a paragraph
    - D. underlining it

Questions 19-25.

DIRECTIONS: Questions 19 through 25 concern the subject of report writing and are based on the information and incidents described in the following paragraph. (In answering these questions, assume that the facts and incidents in the paragraph are true.)

On December 15, at 8 A.M., seven Laborers reported to Foreman Joseph Meehan in the Greenbranch Yard in Queens. Meehan instructed the men to load some 50-pound boxes of books on a truck for delivery to an agency building in Brooklyn. Meehan told the men that, because the boxes were rather heavy, two men should work together, helping each other lift and load each box. Since Michael Harper, one of the Laborers, was without a partner, Meehan helped him with the boxes for a while. When Meehan was called to the telephone in a nearby building, however, Harper decided to lift a box himself. He appeared able to lift the box, but, as he got the box halfway up, he cried out that he had a sharp pain in his back. Another Laborer, Jorge Ortiz, who was passing by, ran over to help Harper put the box down. Harper suddenly dropped the box, which fell on Ortiz' right foot. By this time, Meehan had come out of the building. He immediately helped get the box off Ortiz' foot and had both men lie down. Meehan covered the men with blankets and called an ambulance, which arrived a half hour later. At the hospital, the doctor said that the X-ray results showed that Ortiz' right foot was broken in three places.

19. What would be the BEST term to use in a report describing the injury of Jorge Ortiz?
    A. Strain   B. Fracture   C. Hernia   D. Hemorrhage

    19.____

20. Which of the following would be the MOST accurate summary for the Foreman to put in his report of the incident?
    A. Ortiz attempted to help Harper carry a box which was too heavy for one person, but Harper dropped it before Ortiz got there.
    B. Ortiz tried to help Harper carry a box but Harper got a pain in his back and accidentally dropped the box on Ortiz' foot.
    C. Harper refused to follow Meehan's orders and lifted a box too heavy for him; he deliberately dropped it when Ortiz tried to help him carry it.
    D. Harper lifted a box and felt a pain in his back; Ortiz tried to help Harper put the box down but Harper accidentally dropped it on Ortiz' foot.

    20.____

21. One of the Laborers at the scene of the accident was asked his version of the incident.
    Which information obtained from this witness would be LEAST important for including in the accident report?
    A. His opinion as to the cause of the accident
    B. How much of the accident he saw
    C. His personal opinion of the victims
    D. His name and address

    21.____

22. What should be the MAIN objective of writing a report about the incident described in the above paragraph? To
    A. describe the important elements in the accident situation
    B. recommend that such Laborers as Ortiz be advised not to interfere in another's work unless given specific instructions
    C. analyze the problems occurring when there are not enough workers to perform a certain task
    D. illustrate the hazards involved in performing routine everyday tasks

    22.____

23. Which of the following is information *missing* from the above passage but which *should* be included in a report of the incident? The
    A. name of the Laborer's immediate supervisor
    B. contents of the boxes
    C. time at which the accident occurred
    D. object or action that caused the injury to Ortiz' foot

    23.____

24. According to the description of the incident, the accident occurred because
    A. Ortiz attempted to help Harper who resisted his help
    B. Harper failed to follow instructions given him by Meehan
    C. Meehan was not supervising his men as closely as he should have
    D. Harper was not strong enough to carry the box once he lifted it

    24.____

25. Which of the following is MOST important for a foreman to avoid when writing up an official accident report? 25._____
   A. Using technical language to describe equipment involved in the accident
   B. Putting in details which might later be judged unnecessary
   C. Giving an opinion as to conditions that contributed to the accident
   D. Recommending discipline for employees who, in his opinion, caused the accident

KEY (CORRECT ANSWERS)

1.	B	11.	B
2.	C	12.	B
3.	A	13.	A
4.	B	14.	A
5.	B	15.	C
6.	D	16.	D
7.	C	17.	A
8.	D	18.	B
9.	A	19.	B
10.	C	20.	D

21. C
22. A
23. C
24. B
25. D

TEST 2

DIRECTIONS: Each question or incomplete statement is followed by several suggested answers or completions. Select the one that BEST answers the question or completes the statement. *PRINT THE LETTER OF THE CORRECT ANSWER IN THE SPACE AT THE RIGHT.*

1. Lieutenant X is preparing a report to submit to his commanding officer in order to get approval of a plan of operation he has developed.
   The report starts off with the statement of the problem and continues with the details of the problem. It contains factual information gathered with the help of field and operational personnel. It contains a final conclusion and recommendation for action. The recommendation is supplemented by comments from other precinct staff members on how the recommendations will affect their areas of responsibility. The report also includes directives and general orders ready for the commanding officer's signature. In addition, it has two statements of objections presented by two precinct staff members.
   Which one of the following, if any, is either an item that Lieutenant X should have included in his report and which is not mentioned above, or is an item which Lieutenant X improperly did include in his report?
   A. Considerations of alternative courses of action and their consequences should have been covered in the report.
   B. The additions containing undocumented objections to the recommended course of action should not have been included as part of the report.
   C. A statement on the qualifications of Lieutenant X, which would support his expertness in the field under consideration, should have been included in the report.
   D. The directives and general orders should not have been prepared and included in the report until the commanding officer had approved the recommendations.
   E. None of the above, since Lieutenant X's report was both proper and complete.

1.____

2. During a visit to a section, the district supervisor criticizes the method being used by the assistant foreman to prepare a certain report and orders him to modify the method. This change ordered by the district supervisor is in direct conflict with the specific orders of the foreman.
   In this situation, it would be BEST for the assistant foreman to
   A. change the method and tell the foreman about the change at the first opportunity
   B. change the method and rely on the district supervisor to notify the foreman
   C. report the matter to the foreman and delay the preparation of the report
   D. ask the district supervisor to discuss the matter with the foreman but use the old method for the time being

2.____

3. A department officer should realize that the MOST usual reason for writing a report is to
   A. give orders and follow up their execution
   B. establish a permanent record
   C. raise questions
   D. supply information

4. A very important report which is being prepared by a department officer will soon be due on the desk of the district supervisor. No typing help is available at this time for the officer.
   For the officer to write out this report in longhand in such a situation would be
   A. *bad*; such a report would not make the impression a typed report would
   B. *good*; it is important to get the report in on time
   C. *bad*; the district supervisor should not be required to read longhand reports
   D. *good*; it would call attention to the difficult conditions under which this section must work

5. In a well-written report, the length of each paragraph in the report should be
   A. varied according to the content
   B. not over 300 words
   C. pretty nearly the same
   D. gradually longer as the report is developed and written

6. A clerk in the headquarters office complains to you about the way in which you are filing out a certain report.
   It would be BEST for you to
   A. tell the clerk that you are following official procedures in filling out the report
   B. ask to be referred to the clerk's superior
   C. ask the clerk exactly what is wrong with the way in which you are filling out the report
   D. tell the clerk that you are following the directions of the district supervisor

7. The use of an outline to help in writing a report is
   A. *desirable*, in order to insure good organization and coverage
   B. *necessary*, so it can be used as an introduction to the report itself
   C. *undesirable*, since it acts as a straightjacket and may result in an unbalanced report
   D. *desirable*, if you know your immediate supervisor reads reports with extreme care and attention

8. It is advisable that a department officer do his paper work and report writing as soon as he has completed an inspection MAINLY because
   A. there are usually deadlines to be met
   B. it insures a steady work-flow
   C. he may not have time for this later
   D. the facts are then freshest in his mind

9. Before you turn in a report you have written of an investigation that you have made, you discover some additional information you didn't know about before. Whether or not you re-write the report to include this additional information should depend MAINLY on the
    A. amount of time remaining before the report is due
    B. established policy of the department covering the subject matter of the report
    C. bearing this information will have on the conclusions of the report
    D. number of people who will eventually review the report

10. When a supervisory officer submits a periodic report to the district supervisor, he should realize that the CHIEF importance of such a report is that it
    A. is the principal method of checking on the efficiency of the supervisor and his subordinates
    B. is something to which frequent reference will be made
    C. eliminates the need for any personal follow-up or inspection by higher echelons
    D. permits the district supervisor to exercise his functions of direction, supervision, and control better

11. Conclusions and recommendations are usually placed at the end rather than at the beginning of a report because
    A. the person preparing the report may decide to change some of the conclusions and recommendations before he reaches the end of the report
    B. they are the most important part of the report
    C. they can be judged better by the person to whom the report is sent after he reads the facts and investigators which come earlier in the report
    D. they can be referred to quickly when needed without reading the rest of the report

12. The use of the same method of record-keeping and reporting by all agency sections is
    A. *desirable*, MAINLY because it saves time in section operations
    B. *undesirable*, MAINLY because it kills the initiative of the individual section foreman
    C. *desirable*, MAINLY because it will be easier for the administrator to evaluate and compare section operations
    D. *undesirable*, MAINLY because operations vary from section to section and uniform record-keeping and reporting is not appropriate

13. The GREATEST benefit the section officer will have from keeping complete and accurate records and reports of section operations is that
    A. he will find it easier to run his section efficiently
    B. he will need less equipment
    C. he will need less manpower
    D. the section will run smoothly when he is out

14. You have prepared a report to your superior and are ready to send it forward. But on re-reading it, you think some parts are not clearly expressed and your superior ay have difficulty getting your point.
Of the following, it would be BEST for you to
    A. give the report to one of your men to read, and if he has no trouble understanding it send it through
    B. forward the report and call your superior the next day to ask whether it was all right
    C. forward the report as is; higher echelons should be able to understand any report prepared by a section officer
    D. do the report over, re-writing the sections you are in doubt about

15. The BEST of the following statements concerning reports is that
    A. a carelessly written report may give the reader an impression of inaccuracy
    B. correct grammar and English are unimportant if the main facts are given
    C. every man should be required to submit a daily work report
    D. the longer and more wordy a report is, the better it will read

16. In writing a report, the question of whether or not to include certain material could be determined BEST by considering the
    A. amount of space the material will occupy in the report
    B. amount of time to be spent in gathering the material
    C. date of the material
    D. value of the material to the superior who will read the report

17. Suppose you are submitting a fairly long report to your superior.
The one of the following sections that should come FIRST in this report is a
    A. description of how you gathered material
    B. discussion of possible objections to your recommendations
    C. plan of how your recommendations can be put into practice
    D. statement of the problem dealt with

Questions 18-20.

DIRECTIONS: A foreman is asked to write a report on the incident described in the following passage. Answer Questions 18 through 20 based on the following information.

On March 10, Henry Moore, a laborer, was in the process of transferring some equipment from the machine shop to the third floor. He was using a dolly to perform this task and, as he was wheeling the material through the machine shop, laborer Bob Greene called to him. As Henry turned to respond to Bob, he jammed the dolly into Larry Mantell's leg, knocking Larry down in the process and causing the heavy drill that Larry was holding to fall on Larry's foot. Larry started rubbing his foot and then, infuriated, jumped up and punched Henry in the jaw. The force of the blow drove Henry's head back against the wall. Henry did not fight back; he appeared to be dazed. An ambulance was called to take Henry to the hospital, and the ambulance attendant told the foreman that it appeared likely that Henry had suffered a concussion. Larry's injuries consisted of some bruises, but he refused medical attention.

18. An adequate report of the above incident should give as minimum information the names of the persons involved, the names of the witnesses, the date and the time that each event took place, and the
    A. names of the ambulance attendants
    B. names of all the employees working in the machine shop
    C. location where the accident occurred
    D. nature of the previous safety training each employee had been given

19. The only one of the following which is NOT a fact is
    A. Bob called to Henry
    B. Larry suffered a concussion
    C. Larry rubbed his foot
    D. the incident took place in the machine shop

20. Which of the following would be the MOST accurate summary of the incident for the foreman to put in his report of the accident?
    A. Larry Mantell punched Henry Moore because a drill fell on his foot and he was angry. Then Henry fell and suffered a concussion.
    B. Henry Moore accidentally jammed a dolly into Larry Mantell's foot, knocking Larry down. Larry punched Henry, pushing him into the wall and causing him to bang his head against the wall.
    C. Bob Greene called Henry Moore. A dolly than jammed into Larry Mantell and knocked him down. Larry punched Henry who tripped and suffered some bruises. An ambulance was called.
    D. A drill fell on Larry Mantell's foot. Larry jumped up suddenly and punched Henry Moore and pushed him into the wall. Henry may have suffered a concussion as a result of falling.

Questions 21-25.

DIRECTIONS: Questions 21 through 25 are to be answered ONLY on the basis of the information provided in the following passage.

A written report is a communication of information from one person to another. It is an account of some matter especially investigated, however routine that matter may be. The ultimate basis of any good written report is facts, which become known through observation and verification. Good written reports may seem to be no more than general ideas and opinions. However, in such cases, the facts leading to these opinions were gathered, verified, and reported earlier, and the opinions are dependent upon these facts. Good style, proper form, and emphasis cannot make a good written report out of unreliable information and bad judgment; but, on the other hand, solid investigation and brilliant thinking are not likely to become very useful until they are effectively communicated to others. If a person's work calls for written reports, then his work is often no better than his written reports.

21. Based on the information in the above passage, it can be concluded that opinions expressed in a report should be
    A. based on facts which are gathered and reported
    B. emphasized repeatedly when they result from a special investigation
    C. kept to a minimum
    D. separated from the body of the report

22. In the above passage, the one of the following which is mentioned as a way of establishing facts is
    A. authority
    B. communication
    C. reporting
    D. verification

23. According to the above passage, the characteristic shared by ALL written reports is that they are
    A. accounts of routine matters
    B. transmissions of information
    C. reliable and logical
    D. written in proper form

24. Which of the following conclusions can logically be drawn from the information given in the above passage?
    A. Brilliant thinking can make up for unreliable information in a report.
    B. One method of judging an individual's work is the quality of the written reports he is required to submit.
    C. Proper form and emphasis can make a good report out of unreliable information.
    D. Good written reports that seem to be no more than general ideas should be rewritten.

25. Which of the following suggested titles would be MOST appropriate for this passage?
    A. Gathering and Organizing Facts
    B. Techniques of Observation
    C. Nature and Purpose of Reports
    D. Reports and Opinions: Differences and Similarities

KEY (CORRECT ANSWERS)

1.	A		11.	C
2.	A		12.	C
3.	D		13.	A
4.	B		14.	D
5.	A		15.	A
6.	C		16.	D
7.	A		17.	D
8.	D		18.	C
9.	C		19.	B
10.	D		20.	B

21.	A
22.	D
23.	B
24.	B
25.	C

TEST 3

DIRECTIONS: Each question or incomplete statement is followed by several suggested answers or completions. Select the one that BEST answers the question or completes the statement. *PRINT THE LETTER OF THE CORRECT ANSWER IN THE SPACE AT THE RIGHT.*

Questions 1-5.

DIRECTIONS: The following is an accident report similar to those used in departments for reporting accidents. Questions 1 through 5 are be answered using ONLY the information given in this report.

ACCIDENT REPORT

FROM: John Doe	DATE OF REPORT: June 23	
TITLE: Sanitation Worker		
DATE OF ACCIDENT: June 22 time 3 ~~AM~~ PM	CITY: Metropolitan	
PLACE: 1489 Third Avenue		
VEHICLE NO. 1	VEHICLE NO. 2	
OPERATOR: John Doe, Sanitation Worker Title	OPERATOR: Richard Roe	
VEHICLE CODE NO: 14-238	ADDRESS: 498 High Street	
LICENSE NO.: 0123456	OWNER: Henry Roe ADDRESS: 786 E.83 St.	LIC. NO.: 5N1492
DESCRIPTION OF ACCIDENT: Light green Chevrolet sedan while trying to pass drove in to rear side of sanitation truck which had stopped to collect garbage. No one was injured but there was property damage.		
NATURE OF DAMAGE TO PRIVATE VEHICLE: Right front fender crushed, bumper bent		
DAMAGE TO CITY VEHICLE: Front of left rear fender pushed in. Paint scraped.		
NAME OF WITNESS: Frank Brown	ADDRESS: 48 Kingsway	
SIGNATURE OF PERSON MAKING THIS REPORT *John Doe*	BADGE NO.: 428	

1. Of the following, the one which has been omitted from this accident report is the
    A. location of the accident
    B. drivers of the vehicles involved
    C. traffic situation at the time of the accident
    D. owners of the vehicles involved

    1._____

2. The address of the driver of Vehicle No. 1 is not required because he
    A. is employed by the department
    B. is not the owner of the vehicle
    C. reported the accident
    D. was injured in the accident

    2._____

3. The report indicates that the driver of Vehicle No. 2 was PROBABLY
    A. passing on the wrong side of the truck
    B. not wearing his glasses
    C. not injured in the accident
    D driving while intoxicated

    3._____

2 (#3)

4. The number of people *specifically* referred to in this report is
   A. 3 B. 4 C. 5 D. 6

5. The license number of Vehicle No. 1 is
   A. 428 B. 5N1492 C. 14-238 D. 0123456

6. In a report of unlawful entry into department premises, it is LEAST important to include the
   A. estimated value of the property missing
   B. general description of the premises
   C. means used to get into the premises
   D. time and date of entry

7. In a report of an accident, it is LEAST important to include the
   A. name of the insurance company of the person injured in the accident
   B. probable cause of the accident
   C. time and place of the accident
   D. names and addresses of all witnesses of the accident

8. Of the following, the one which is NOT required in the preparation of a weekly functional expense report is the
   A. hourly distribution of the time by proper heading in accordance with the actual work performed
   B. signatures of officers not involved in the preparation of the report
   C. time records of the men who appear on the payroll of the respective locations
   D. time records of men working in other districts assigned to this location

KEY (CORRECT ANSWERS)

1. C   5. D
2. A   6. B
3. C   7. A
4. B   8. B

LEGAL ASPECTS OF A HOUSING INSPECTION

CONTENTS

	Page
I. Introduction	1
II. Entry	1
III. Search Warrant	2
IV. Evidence	3
V. Model Ordinance Solutions	3
VI. Legal Aspects of the APHA-CDC Recommended Ordinance	4
VII. The Inspector as a Witness	5

LEGAL ASPECTS OF A HOUSING INSPECTION

I. Introduction

The state may regulate the use and enjoyment of individual property for the good of its citizens. Such regulation does not usually conflict with the constitutional protections given to the owner or occupant of property. The right of the state (or municipality as the state's delegate) to enact and enforce a housing code is based on the state's police power. This general authority has never been precisely defined, but it has recently been called "The power inherent in a Government to enact laws within Constitutional limits to protect the order, safety, health, morals, and general welfare of society."[1]

Courts have pointed out that municipalities may properly impose restrictions on individual property owners when these restrictions are needed for the protection of the public health, safety, or welfare.

What can be done in the name of the public health, safety, and welfare may be better understood if one surveys a few cases in which housing code provisions have been held constitutional. Provisions in ordinances requiring windows and ventilation,[2] screens,[3] maintenance of hot water,[4] and many other necessities and amenities of life have been upheld,[5] even though these ordinances interfere with the rights of ownership of property and in spite of the costs to the owner for repair, installation, alteration, or demolition that can often be compelled by the law.

The substantive portions of local housing codes (that define what can or cannot be done) have been generally upheld by the courts; in the area of implementation, however, difficulties have been encountered. A just balance between the rights of the individual and the needs of each community is the goal towards which each person charged with the protection of the public health should strive. The right of an inspector to entry, the necessity and requirements of a search warrant, and the admissibility of evidence obtained in a search are three grey areas of indecision.

II. Entry

The Fourth Amendment guarantees people the right to privacy — the right to shut one's door against officials of the state unless under proper authority of law. Concepts and procedures that previously guided the conduct of housing, sanitation, and safety inspection programs in this country have been reexamined and revised in recent decisions of the Supreme Court of the United States.[6,7] When clear and specific consent to enter premises has been freely and intentionally given, an inspector may enter the premises.

Entry on and inspection of private property (no distinction is made between residential and commercial property not open to the public) by government officials without proper consent, however, is an "unreasonable search and seizure" within the Fourth Amendment and may not be enforced unless authorized by a valid search warrant.[8]

Searches for housing violations by an agent of an administrative agency are considered significant intrusions of the interests that are protected by the Fourth Amendment[9] against arbitrary invasions by government officials and by the Fourteenth Amendment against state officials.[10] The occupant, therefore, may not be punished for refusing to permit a warrantless inspection.

Consent to inspect may, however, be given. Constitutional rights protected by the Fourth and Fifth Amendments may be voluntarily waived,[11] but there is a distinction between submission and the kind of consent that is necessary to constitute a voluntary waiver. Officers cannot demand admission to private premises in the name of the law or "under color of office;"[12] such entry has been said to be granted "in submission to authority rather than as an understanding and intentional waiver of a constitutional right."[13] In short, the consent must be clear and specific, freely and intentionally given. Where a search alleged to be based on consent is challenged, courts have required evidence showing that the consent was given in the knowledge that the occupant has the right to refuse such consent with impunity.[14] and the Government, then, has the burden of proving by clear and positive evidence, that such consent has been given.[15]

Evidence of consent may be oral or written, and experience in the inspection field will show which is preferable. The Department of Justice "Handbook of the Law of Search and Seizure (1967)" recommends that the consent be in writing. The legal office for each housing agency should provide a form that will be suitable for its jurisdiction.

Where a verbal consent is relied on, some Federal courts have held that nothing short of a statement by the inspector advising the person of his right to refuse a warrantless search will meet the Fourth Amendment requirements that a person must knowingly waive his rights.[16]

III. Search Warrant

Since it has been decided that, without consent, a search warrant is necessary to support the entry, the question arises: Is there an available procedure for obtaining a search warrant to make an inspection? The Supreme Court recognized that the only effective way to have all premises comply with the minimum standards required by municipal codes is through routine periodic inspection of all structures.[17] The area-inspection approach (a plan for systematic inspection, from time to time, of structures contained within a continguous area) is considered to be a reasonable search of private property within the meaning of the Fourth Amendment. A warrant for an inspection of residential or commercial premises need not be based on reasonable cause to believe that a violation exists in the premises sought to be inspected, but can be based on reasonableness of need to conduct periodic, area-wide inspection, based on the passage of time, the nature of the building (e.g., a multifamily apartment house), or the condition of the entire area.*

The recent Supreme Court decision stated the following guidelines for determination of "probable cause" to issue a warrant:

"... it is obvious that probable cause to issue a warrant to inspect must exist if reasonable legislative or administrative standards for conducting an area inspection are satisfied with respect to a particular dwelling. Such standards, which will vary with the municipal program being enforced, may be based upon the passage of time, the nature of the building (e.g., a multifamily apartment house) or the condition of the entire area, but they will not necessarily depend upon specific knowledge of the condition of the particular dwelling."

Although the Fourth Amendment bars warrantless, nonemergency inspection of residential and commercial premises without the occupant's consent, the Supreme Court noted that:[17]

1. Prompt inspection, even without a warrant, is possible in emergency situations.[18]

2. Since there is no compelling urgency to inspect at a particular time on a particular day in most routine area inspections, as a practical matter and in light of the Fourth Amendment's requirement that a warrant specify the property to be searched, "it seems likely that warrants should normally be sought only after entry is refused, unless there has been a citizen complaint or there is other satisfactory reason for securing immediate entry."

3. "... the requirement of a warrant procedure does not suggest any change in what seems to be the prevailing local policy in most situations, of authorizing entry, but not entry by force, to inspect."

The Fourth Amendment requirement that a search warrant particularly describe the "thing to be seized" may occasion some difficulty for general housing and sanitation inspections that can extend from defective appliances, hazardous conditions, and cleanliness to window screens, rat holes, and the number of electrical outlets in a room. Such a broad-ranging inspection may require a thorough search of every room in an apartment, or entire commercial premises, as well as closets, cupboards, storerooms, and related accounts and records. Rather than specify in detail every item to which the inspection will be directed, statements should be sufficient that will permit the court issuing the warrant to determine necessity for the warrant and determine the limits of the search, e.g., inspection of the physical condition of the premises, plumbing, electrical wiring and fixtures, and related conditions bearing on violations of sections _____ of the Housing Code (and of sections _____ of the regulations issued

---

*The matter of "blanket warrants" is one that has not been fully qualified. Until the time that guidelines pertaining to the use of blanket search warrants are established, localities are cautioned to consult with their legal advisers before proceeding in this matter.

thereunder). It may also be desirable to attach to the warrant copies of the cited sections of the code.

If the occupant of premises to be searched refused to comply with a warrant, how is the warrant to be enforced?

When entry under a search warrant is refused, the court can punish such refusal. In addition, the provisions in most housing codes that penalize refusal to comply with or resistance to the execution of the provisions of the code probably would be adequate to support a penalty for refusal to comply with a lawful search warrant issued to implement the inspection provisions. Entry by force, the traditional method of enforcing compliance with a warrant, is used to seize criminal evidence that may be disposed of or secreted if entry is delayed; in the case of housing violations, however, hiding the violations from the inspector actually results in giving the occupant time to correct the defects. Delay, except in the case of emergencies, does not ordinarily frustrate the public interest.

IV. Evidence

A person, then, has the right not only to refuse a warrantless entry (under the Fourth Amendment) but also may resist unauthorized entry designed to secure evidence that may be used to deprive him of life, liberty, or property (under the Fifth Amendment).

What use may be made of evidence obtained in the course of a search or inspection that is conducted without a warrant or without probable cause to believe that a local code has been violated? One result is that any seizure made during an illegal search would itself be illegal;[19] if timely and appropriate objection is made, such evidence may not be used or remain in evidence.[20] Such evidence may not be employed in state criminal proceedings.[21] Physical, tangible materials obtained either during or as a direct result of an unlawful search are barred from trial, and intangible evidence, such as a verbal statement made during an illegal search[22] and testimony concerning objects illegally observed.[23]

The applicability of this rule emphasized the importance of establishing clearly that consent has been obtained for a warrantless search based on consent.

V. Model Ordinance Solutions

The Housing Act of 1954 required that any city applying for Federal urban renewal assistance must have a plan for code enforcement as part of its workable program. Before passage of the Act, few cities had enacted such a code; in the ensuing few years, more than 650 cities have enacted such codes. The "APHA-CDC Recommended Housing Maintenance and Occupancy Ordinance" (a model ordinance) seeks to provide solutions to some of these areas that have been discussed.

Section XI of the "APHA-CDC Recommended Housing Maintenance and Occupancy Ordinance" states the procedures needed for a housing inspection. These procedures serve the dual purposes of informing the public of the nature of the program of inspection and of making many inspection procedures routine for the officers who carry out the provisions of the ordinance. One requirement is that the inspector provide the householder with identification and a copy of both the plan of inspection and an individual schedule of the areas and facilities to be inspected; this is an attempt to protect against unauthorized intrusions by strangers.

An area-wide inspection is more effective when the enforcing officer obtains consent to such inspection whenever possible. The model ordinance states that inspections will be made between the hours of 8:00 a.m. and 5:00 p.m., or by appointment arranged between the enforcing officer and the householder. Before an inspection is conducted, the inspector must present his credentials and a schedule of the areas and facilities he wants to survey. If the inspection is to be conducted on an area-wide basis, a copy of a plan for neighborhood inspection authorized by the agency responsible for the enforcement activities is to be shown to the householder. Before these neighborhood inspections are undertaken, cooperation is sought through consultations with organizations representative of the neighborhood residents, where these exist.

To impose penalties against those who interfere with routine inspections, an ordinance must clearly set forth the duty of the owner, occupant, or other person in charge to admit the inspector and must clearly spell out the nature of the punishment to be imposed if this requirement is violated.[24] The APHA-CDC Recommended Ordinance creates civil penalties for violation of its provisions (Section XV) and provides that the owner, occupant, or other person in charge shall give entry and free access; if this is refused or interfered with, an order from a competent court can be sought ordering the person in charge to cease and desist such interference.

Section XI [21, 27] of the APHA-CDC Recommended Ordinance specifically provides that evidence obtained in the course of inspection shall not be admissible in any administrative or judicial proceeding not related to the housing code, unless the householder consents to such use. This is an attempt to minimize the difficulties surrounding the use of evidence obtained without a warrant or probable cause. "Such evidence shall be considered privileged, and shall not be admissible in any judicial proceeding, without the consent of the owner, occupant, or other person in charge of the dwelling unit or rooming unit so inspected."

VI. Legal Aspects of the APHA-CDC Recommended Ordinance

The Section XIV[25] outlines procedures to be followed after violations of the housing ordinance have been found. The housing codes of most municipalities generally contain similar provisions. These procedures are summarized below:

Notice of violation is given when the premises fail to meet the ordinance requirements. This notice, in writing, sets forth the alleged violation, describes where the alleged violation has been committed, and provides a reasonable, specified time for correction. The owner, occupant, or other person in charge of the premises or other proper person, as described in the ordinance, is served with this notice personally or by registered mail. Although it does not constitute "legal notice," ordinary mail can generally be used for first notices. If the person cannot be found, service may be made by posting notice on the premises or by publication in a newspaper of general circulation[26] for the specified time.

After the reasonable time for correction has elapsed, the premises are reinspected, and if the violations have not been corrected, a second notice of violation is issued. This second notice is an order requiring that the person served with such notice, if not requesting reconsideration of petitioning for a hearing (Section XVIII), correct the failure to meet ordinance requirements within a reasonable specified time.

After expiration of the specified, reasonable time or after a final decision (Section XVIII, model ordinance) has been rendered against the person served, this second notice can be recorded in the registry of deeds so that all subsequent transferees of title to the premises are considered to have notice of the continuing existence of the violations and are liable to all the same penalties.

Civil penalties[21, 27] (Section XV) are provided in the form of fines, or jail terms, or both after a reasonable period, but not while reconsideration, hearing, or appeal is pending.

Repairs[28] (Section XVI) may be made by the appropriate authorized agency if they are not made by the owner or person in charge and if failure to make them will endanger public health, safety, or welfare. As specified in the model ordinance, the cost of repairs, not to exceed 50 per cent of the market value of the structure, is a debt in favor of the agency and is recoverable in a civil action if not paid.[29]

Demolition[30] (Section XVI) of a structure can be ordered if it is unfit for human habitation and does not warrant repair. If the owner does not remove the structure within a reasonable time after notice, the agency may have it removed, chargeable to the owner, on receiving approval of a demolition order from a competent court. Pending removal of the structure, the owner cannot allow a voluntarily vacated building to be reoccupied.[31] The excavation must be refilled.[32]

A revolving fund[33] (Section XVI) is created from funds from penalties, license fees, judgments collected, grants, loans, gifts, and other sources[34] to support the cost of repairs and demolition.

Collection and dissemination of information[35] (Section XVII) concerning techniques of maintenance, repair, and sanitation and the requirements of the housing ordinance are authorized.

An application for reconsideration (Section XVIII) may be applied for by a person aggrieved by a notice or order requiring repair or demolition. At an informal conference[36] with the appropriate authorized agency, the applicant can present his grounds for believing that the order should be revoked or modified; the agency then advises the applicant whether or not it will modify or set aside the order.

A hearing[37] (Section XVIII) (for use with this reconsideration procedure) may be petitioned for by an aggrieved person with the Hearing Agency.[38] At this time, the petitioner is given an opportunity to show cause why the notice or order should be modified or withdrawn, or the time extended for compliance. The Hearing Agency has the power to affirm, modify, revoke, or extend the time for compliance of the order or notice and may also grant variances from the provisions of the ordinance (or rules and regulations issued pursuant to the ordinance) if such variance is in harmony with the general purpose of the ordinance to secure public health, safety, and welfare.

A formal conference[36] (Section XVIII) is provided as an alternative to the above described "application for reconsideration" and "hearing." The formal conference procedure provides for the aggrieved person to petition, by letter, setting forth his grounds for contesting the notice or order. The agency sets the time and designates one or more referees to preside at the conference. The referee is authorized to administer oaths and subpoena witnesses or documents. A verbatim record is kept of the conference. The petitioner is then notified of the decision in writing.

A hearing[37] (Section XVIII) (for use with this formal conference procedure) allows the aggrieved person to protest, by petition to the Hearing Agency, the decision of the referee. The Hearing Agency notifies the petitioner and the appropriate authorizing agency of the hearing and requests a transcript of the formal conference. After the hearing, which is conducted on the basis of the verbatim record kept at the formal conference, the Hearing Agency notifies the petitioner of its decision to affirm, modify, revoke, extend compliance time, or grant variances.

Appeal[39] (Section XVIII) from the final decision of the Hearing Agency may be made by the aggrieved person by filing a petition with a court of competent jurisdiction asking that the decision be set aside in whole or in part. This petition is given to the Hearing Agency, which files a record of the proceedings upon which it based its decision. The court then affirms, modifies, or vacates the decision of the Hearing Agency. The findings of the Hearing Agency on questions of fact are sustained if they are supported by substantial evidence on the record, considered as a whole.

VII. The Inspector as a Witness

On those few occasions when appeal from the final decision of the Hearing Agency is made by the aggrieved person to a court of competent jurisdiction, the housing inspector, as part of his duties, will be required to appear as a witness in a court trial. As a witness, the inspector will be called on to relate facts that he has observed and to testify concerning evidence he has gathered in connection with the alleged violation. An inspector should be familiar with courtroom proceedings so that his testimony will effectively present information he has gathered for his agency.

The attorney that represents the housing agency will, properly, discuss the case with the inspector in advance of the trial. This will be the attorney's opportunity to determine what the inspector knows about the case and to indicate the type, kind, and amount of evidence that the attorney will need and that the inspector will be able to supply. At this time, the inspector can also properly ask the attorney about any courtroom procedures of which he is in doubt.

The inspector may be called on to present his testimony in a pretrial deposition. The attorney for the aggrieved party can require the inspector to appear for oral questioning in advance of the trial to obtain oral answers recorded in writing, under oath, concerning the inspector's knowledge of the case. It is the inspector's duty to answer questions asked him in the same manner as if he were in court. The agency's attorney will be present to guide him.

When called as a witness in the court proceedings, the inspector will generally be examined by the attorney for the housing agency on direct examination. The attorney for the opposition then has the opportunity, if he wishes, to ask questions regarding the same information on which the inspector has already testified.

The inspector is to testify to the facts as accurately as possible. Before the court appearance, he should refresh his memory about details of the case, e.g., dates, time, and location and condition of the premises. He should make available to the agency's attorney the most recent and best available evidence. Photographs, correctly labeled, should adequately show the extent of the violations and should be as recent as possible. Because there will not be a future opportunity to submit exhibits, the photographs, maps, or other displays, should be available to the inspector and attorney in the courtroom.

Just as ill-prepared and poor, outdated evidence will leave a poor impression on the court, or the jury, or both, so will a poor unkempt appearance. The inspector, as a witness, should be neat and clean. His demeanor on the witness stand will add import to his testimony. The following suggestions* will help to make more effective the information that the inspector is prepared to give:

1. **Never Lose Your Temper.** If a witness loses his temper, he places himself at the mercy of the cross-examiner. He appears to be prejudiced, and judges and juries are not interested in prejudiced testimony. They are interested only in the facts. Keep your temper, and your service as a witness will be more pleasant. Your testimony will be more valuable.

2. **Be Attentive.** You must be alert at all times you are in the witness chair so that you can hear, understand, and give a proper and intelligent

---

*Reproduced with permission of the Ohio State Bar Association, Copyright 1957, 1964.

answer to each question. If the judge or jury gets the impression you are indifferent, they may not believe your story.

3 **Think Before You Speak.** Hasty and thoughtless answers may be incorrect and may cause problems. This is particularly true when the opposing lawyer is cross-examining. He may ask you leading questions — questions which suggest only one answer. Make sure you understand the question; then give it an accurate answer to the best of your ability. If you do not know the answer, say so.

4 **Speak Clearly.** There is nothing more annoying to a court, jury, and lawyers as a witness who refuses to speak clearly enough to be heard. An inaudible voice not only detracts from the value of your testimony, but it also tends to make the court and jury think that you are not certain of what you are saying. Everyone in the courtroom is entitled to know what you have to say. There are no secrets in court; the court reporter who is recording the proceedings must be able to hear all your testimony.

5 **If You Don't Understand A Question, Ask That It Be Explained.** Many times, a witness will not understand a question that has been asked but will try to answer it. This is confusing to the court, the jury, and the lawyers. It also extends the time a witness will be on the witness stand because the lawyers must go back and correct any misinformation given by the witness who does not understand the question. If you do not understand the particular question, do not hesitate to say so and ask that the question be explained. It will save time and confusion.

6 **Answer All Questions Directly.** Too often, a witness will be so anxious to tell his story that he will want to get it all told in answer to the first question. Listen to the question. If you can answer it with a "yes" or "no," do so. Never volunteer information. The information which you volunteer may have no bearing on the case and may serve only to delay the proceedings.

7 **Stick To The Facts.** Don't guess or speculate. The only thing that you will be permitted to testify to is what you personally know. What you *know* is important. What you *think* is unimportant.

8 **Be Helpful, Not Funny.** A trial is an important matter to the parties involved. Their money, property, or freedom may be lost by your testimony. Don't try to be a wit.

REFERENCES

1 *Lees v. Bay Area Pollution Control District*, 48 Ca. Rptr. 295, 299, (1965).

2 *Richards v. City of Columbia*, 227 S.C. 538, 88 S.E. 2d (1955).

3 *Paquette v. City of Fall River*, 338 Mass. 368, 155 N.E. 2d 775 (1959).

4 *Danker v. City of New York*, 194 N.Y.S. 2d 975 (1959).

5 See, generally, *The Constitutionality of Housing Codes*, National Association of Housing and Redevelopment Officials, (2d. Ed. 1964).

6 *Camera v. Municipal Court of the City and County of San Francisco*, 87 S. Ct. 1727 (1967).

7 *See v. City of Seattle*, 87 S. Ct. 1937 (1967).

8 Ibid.

9 The Fourth Amendment (U.S. Constitution) provides:
"The right of the people to be secure in their persons, houses, papers, and effects, against unreasonable searches and seizures, shall not be violated, and no Warrants shall issue, but upon probable cause, supported by Oath or affirmation, and particularly describing the place to be searched, and the persons or things to be seized."

10 *Ker v. California*, 374 U.S. 23, 30 (1963); *Wolf v. Colorado*, 338 U.S. 25, 27 (1949); *Mapp v. Ohio*, 367 U.S. 643 (1961).

11 *Zap v. United States*, 328 U.S. 624, 628 (1946).

12 *Amos v. United States*, 255 U.S. 313 (1921); *Johnson v. United States*, 333 U.S. 10, 13 (1948).

13 333 U.S. at 13; *United States v. Smith*, 2 Cir., 1962, 308 F 2d 657, 663.

14 *Judd v. United States*, D.C. Cir. 1951, 190F. 2d 649, 651; *Robbins v. MacKenzie*, 1 Cir., 1966, 364 F. 2d 45, 49, cert. den.; *United States v. Como*, 2 Cir., 1955, 340 F 2d 891.

15 *McDonald v. United States*, 10 Cir., 1962, 307 F 2d 272; *Judd v. United States, supra; Simmons v. Bomar*, 6 Cir., 1965, 349 F 2d 365, 366. *Kovach v. United States*, 6 Cir., 1931, 53 F 2d 639; *Channel v. United States*, 9 Cir., 1960, 285 F 2d 217, 219 cf. *Parrish v. Civil Service Comm. of County Alameda*, 57 Cal. Rptr. 623 (1967).

16 *United States v. Blalock*, 255 F. Supp. 268 (1966); *United States v. Nickrasch*, 7 Cir., 1966, 367 F. 2d 740, 744.

Contra: *Gorman v. United States*, 1 Cir., 1967, 36 L.W. 2039 which held a specific Fourth Amendment warning unnecessary in the following factual situation:

> "When the accused is directly asked whether he objects to the search, there must be at least some suggestion that his objection is significant, or that the search waits on his consent. When this is combined with a warning of his right to counsel, which would seem in the circumstances to put him on notice that he can refuse to cooperate, we think it fair to infer that his purported consent is in fact voluntary."

17 Supra, footnote 6

18 The opinion cites *North American Cold Storage Co. v. City of Chicago*, 211 U.S. 306 (seizure of unwholesome foods); *Jacobson v. Massachusetts*, 197 U.S. 11 (compulsory smallpox vaccination); *Compagnie Francaise v. Board of Health*, 186 U.S. 380 (health quarantine); *Kroplin v. Truax*, 119 Ohio St. 610, 165 N.E. 498 (summary destruction of tubercular cattle).

19 Evidence obtained in reinspections, as well as in initial inspections of a tenant's rooms, cannot be gathered for use against the tenant solely on the basis of the landlord's consent to a search, where the penalties to be imposed are of a criminal or quasi-criminal nature. See *Chapman vs. United States*, 365 U.S. 610 (1961), where a landlord gave police officers entry to defendant's rented house wherein he maintained an illegal still. The evidence obtained in the search was declared inadmissible by the Supreme Court. Where the obligation to be enforced is that of the landlord as opposed to the tenant, the landlord's consent to inspection of the tenant's dwelling, dwelling unit or rooming unit is, of course, binding upon him.

20 *Weeks v. United States*, 232 U.S. 383 (1914); *Silverthorne Lumber Co. v. United States*, 251 U.S. 385, 391-392 (1920); *Boyd v. United States*, 116 U.S. 616, 630 (1886).

21 A continuing controversy exists as to whether evidence gathered in a health inspection made without a warrant may be employed against an offending owner, occupant, or other person in charge of the inspected structure. *Mapp vs. Ohio*, 367 U.S. 643 (1961), established that evidence obtained in a search in violation of the Fourth Amendment's proscription against unreasonable search and seizures may not be employed in State criminal proceedings, through the operation of the Fourteenth Amendment's Due Process Clause.

The proposed ordinance creates civil penalties for violation of its provisions. But courts are beginning to apply the exclusionary rule of *Mapp* to quasi-criminal and civil proceedings, as well as in criminal prosecutions. In *One 1958 Plymouth Sedan vs. Pennsylvania*, 380 U.S. 693 (1965), State liquor enforcement officers, without a warrant, stopped and searched defendant's automobile and found 31 cases of liquor therein. The state filed a petition for forfeiture of the car, a civil proceeding. The Pennsylvania State Supreme Court upheld the action, stating that the exclusionary rule applies in criminal cases only. The United States Supreme Court reversed, holding that evidence obtained by means of a search in violation of the Fourth Amendment may not be relied upon by the State, under the prohibition of the Fourteenth Amendment, to sustain a forfeiture. A forfeiture under these circumstances could lead to even greater penalties than an impermissible criminal prosecution. Such an anomalous situation, said the Court, must not be permitted to occur.

In *Incorporated Village of Laurel Hollow vs. Laverne Originals*, 171 N.Y. 2d 900, 218 NYS 2d 703 (1966), the New York Court of Appeals held that evidence obtained by a village building inspector in the course of an illegal search was improperly received in a civil contempt proceeding to impose a fine, since although the penalty was civil, such proceeding could impose a basically penal sanction.

In *Carson vs. State*, 221 Gs. 299, 144 S.E. 2d 384 (1965), an action was brought to abate gambling as a public nuisance. The Supreme Court of Georgia applied the rules of *Mapp* and *One 1958 Plymouth Sedan* in stating that the warrants in the case were issued without a showing of probable cause and that the evidence, therefore, must be excluded.

Two very recent cases have applied the exclusionary rule to evidence illegally obtained by private individuals in divorce proceedings. In *Williams vs. Williams*, 8 Ohio Misc. 156, (Common Pleas, Clermont County 1966), it was stated that the *Mapp* rule applies equally to civil cases and a motion for a new trial will not be granted when based upon evidence obtained in an illegal search and seizure. And in *Del Presto vs. Del Presto*, 92 N.J. Super, 305, 223 A. 2d 217, (1966), a New Jersey court held that evidence seized by forcible illegal entry of a correspondent's home was inadmissible in a divorce case, and recounted the development of the exclusionary rule from its announcement to the present.

22 *Wong Sun v. United States*, 371 U.S. 471, 484-486 (1963); *Silverman v. United States*, 365 U.S. 505 (1961).

23 *McGinnis v. United States*, 1 Cir. 1955, 227 F. 2d 598, 603.

24 In *City of Saint Louis vs. Evans*, 337 S.W. 2d 918 (Sup. Ct. Mo. 1960), an ordinance empowered inspectors to enter between 9 a.m. and 6 p.m. and to obtain police assistance if admission was refused. Defendant did refuse such admission, and an officer was summoned. The defendant still refused entry. The Supreme Court of Missouri reversed the defendant's conviction, citing the failure of the ordinance to set forth a specific duty to admit or a specific penalty for those refusing admission. The Court did remand, however, for further proceedings relative to a related charge, interfering with an officer in the performance of his official duties.

In *District of Columbia v. Little*, 339 U.S. 1 (1949), a mere refusal to admit was held no violation of a regulation prohibiting one from interfering with or preventing inspections. The Court found no duty to assist the inspection officers, but only a proscription against actual physical obstruction of them by means of force. From this case, and others like it, it is concluded that ordinances must clearly provide for penalties for refusal to admit inspectors.

25 This section is intended to comply with constitutional requirements of due process. As was said in *Hoehamer v. Village of Elmwood Park*, 361 Ill. 423, 198 N.E. 345 (1932),

> "An orderly proceeding in which a person is served with notice, actual or constructive, and has an opportunity to be heard and to protect and enforce his rights before a court having power to hear and determine the cause is due process of law."

26 The service of notice by newspaper publication is optional unless otherwise required by law. Larger jurisdictions may find it easier to meet the cost of such publication than will smaller communities.

27 Civil penalties are proposed in lieu of the more common criminal sanctions. This gives implementation to the recommendations of Judah Gribetz and Frank P. Grad in "Housing Code Enforcement — Sanctions and Remedies," 66 Colum L. Rev. 1254 (1966). The inadequacy and historically demonstrable failure of the criminal sanction portrayed in that article and the plan for a shift toward a cumulative civil penalty are reflected in this ordinance.

28 Repair is designed to replace the more common remedies of placarding, vacating the premises, and receivership. The advantages of repair are that tenants in repairable multiple dwellings are not forced to look for other lodgings and that the authorized agency need not involve itself as a landlord, with buildings to manage, awaiting repairs. The cost of repairs is met both by a potential civil action and through the mechanism of the revolving fund (see Section XVI).

29 Authority for a city, under its police power, to require private action for repair and to recover the cost of work done if the individual required to make the improvement does not act has long been upheld, although it has not been frequently invoked in recent cases. See *City of Independence vs. Purdy*, 46 Iowa 202 (1877), where the city filled in defendant's stagnant pond and was allowed to recover the cost in a private action. The authorization for civil recovery of

30 such costs eliminates the long delay attendant when liens are imposed on property; these liens are mere clouds on the title, generally payable at that indefinite time in the future when the property is transferred.

30 It is well-settled law that municipal ordinances may provide for the condemnation of buildings failing to comply with their provisions. See *City of Nashville v. Weakley*, 170 Tenn. 278, 95 S.W. 2d 37 (1936), in which it was held, among other things, that a property owner has a duty to keep his property in such a state of repair the public is not endangered; when he fails in this duty, the municipality may perform demolition for him, at his expense.

31 The provision prohibiting the owner from permitting reoccupation of a voluntarily vacated dwelling, dwelling unit, or room unit in a structure scheduled for demolition represents an attempt to protect occupants from dangerous conditions, but does not apply the traditional and harsher condition that the structure be vacated forthwith at the time the demolition order is issued. This is an attempt to balance the need of the tenant to find other accommodations with the need to protect the public health, safety, and welfare.

32 The provision requiring filling the below-ground demolition site that remains when an unfit structure has been removed is an obvious, but often neglected, means of protecting the public health and safety.

33 The fund is a necessity where repair and demolition carried on by the adopting jurisdiction are contemplated.

34 The adopting jurisdiction may subsequently provide that tenants' rents may be paid into a court of competent jurisdiction, to be applied against repairs, since it permits the addition of such other revenues to the fund as the adopting jurisdiction finds necessary in its own particular situation.

35 This section grants the responsible agency powers in addition to the mere policing and licensing functions. When desired, the adopting jurisdiction may adopt regulations pursuant to this section that provide for instruction to owners, occupants, and other persons in charge of structures affected by this ordinance in basic techniques of good housekeeping.

36 The conference is designed as the first step to give the aggrieved party a right to be heard. Two alternative methods for holding such conferences are provided so that the adopting jurisdiction may select the procedure most in conformity with its needs and resources. The application for reconsideration is an informal meeting that contemplates powers of persuasion will be brought to bear. Any hearing following such an informal meeting will, of course, be conducted *de novo*, or as a matter of first impression (first presentation to a court for examination). The formal conference procedure is designed as a full inquiry into the petitioner's complaint and calls for a hearing on the record of such conference.

37 The hearing is the second opportunity offered an aggrieved party to be heard. Depending on the type of initial "reconsideration" or "conference" adopted, this may be the first opportunity for the petitioner to state a formal case or this may be a review of a formal proceeding, based entirely on the original record.

38 The use of the term "hearing agency" permits the adopting jurisdiction to make use either of personnel responsible for the day-to-day enforcement of the ordinance, or of an independent hearing unit from outside such agency, at its option.

39 The third and final resort of the aggrieved party is to the courts. This may be through an appeal taken to an existing tribunal, preferably to a special session of that court, designated to hear cases dealing with the residential environment or to a specialized housing court, if one is to be created. The powers and duties of the Housing Court will depend on local law and should be articulated by each adopting jurisdiction to serve its particular needs. If a jurisdiction decides to create a Housing Court, such choice will, of course, be premised on the authority of the adopting jurisdiction to establish courts in general. Where a city desires a Housing Court and only the State has power to establish courts, a separate statute providing for local housing courts will be necessary. This ordinance can be adopted without the creation of such a court, but if a Housing Court is desired, it is suggested that the term "Housing Court" be substituted for "court of competent jurisdiction" in those provisions of this ordinance dealing with imposition and collection of civil penalties, appeals from decisions of the Hearing Agency, and civil actions for the recovery of expenditures made by the jurisdiction in effecting repair or demolition.

40 87 S. Ct at 1736.

THE CONSTITUTION OF THE UNITED STATES

AMENDMENT 4

The right of the people to be secure in their persons, houses, papers, and effects, against unreasonable searches and seizures, shall not be violated, and no Warrants shall issue, but upon probable cause, supported by Oath or affirmation, and particular describing the place to be searched, and the persons or things to be seized.

AMENDMENT 14

Section 1. All persons born or naturalized in the United States, and subject to the jurisdiction thereof, are citizens of the United States and of the State wherein they reside. No State shall make or enforce any law which shall abridge the privileges or immunities of citizens of the United States; nor shall any State deprive any person of life, liberty, or property, without due process of law; nor deny to any person within its jurisdiction the equal protection of the laws.

Section 2. Representatives shall be apportioned among the several States according to their respective numbers, counting the whole number of persons in each State, excluding Indians not taxed. But when the right to vote at any election for the choice of electors for President and Vice President of the United States, Representatives in Congress, the Executive and Judicial officers of a State, or the members of the Legislature thereof, is denied to any of the male inhabitants of such State, being twenty-one years of age, and citizens of the United States, or in any way abridges except for participation in rebellion, or other crime, the basis of representation therein shall be reduced in the proportion which the number of such male citizens shall bear to the whole number of male citizens twenty-one years of age in such State.

Section 3. No person shall be a Senator or Representative in Congress, or elector of President and Vice President, or hold any office, civil or military, under the United States, or under any State, who, having previously taken an oath, as a member of Congress, or as an officer of the United States, or as a member of any State legislature, or as an executive or judicial officer of any State, to support the Constitution of the United States, shall have engaged in insurrection or rebellion against the same, or given aid or comfort to the enemies thereof. But Congress may by a vote of two-thirds of each House, remove such disability.

Section 4. The validity of the public debt of the United States, authorized by law, including debts incurred for payment of pensions and bounties for services in suppressing insurrection or rebellion, shall not be questioned. But neither the United States nor any State shall assume or pay any debt or obligation incurred in aid of insurrection or rebellion against the United States, or any claim for the loss or emancipation of any slave; but all such debts, obligations and claims shall be held illegal and void.

Section 5. The Congress shall have power to enforce, by appropriate legislation, the provision of this article.

HUMAN RELATIONS ASPECTS OF A HOUSING INSPECTION

I. General Considerations

The term "housing inspection" is generally understood to mean a close-up observation of actual conditions that exist in a dwelling and on its premises. It is conducted by a trained, qualified, and competent appointed official to determine whether the observed conditions meet the minimum requirements specified by the local housing ordinance. In cases where the minimum requirements are not met, the inspection procedure offers an opportunity to begin the necessary action to bring the existing conditions up to a level that will be acceptable under provisions of the ordinance.

A. **Purposes of the Housing Inspection**

   For the occupant of the dwelling unit, the inspection should be an opportunity to compare the conditions in which he lives with those considered to be minimal to protect his health and safety. In addition it provides a check on the quality of maintenance given to the facilities of his dwelling unit since the last inspection.

   For the code enforcement or housing improvement agency, the inspection procedure provides a means for:

   1. Gathering data that can be combined with other, similar data to develop a comprehensive picture of housing conditions in the community as an aid to measure improvement progress.

   2. Executing its responsibility for protecting the health and safety of individual citizens as well as the public generally.

   The main focus of the housing agency's activities should be primarily related to the improvement of the housing quality of the community rather than to the mere enforcement of a housing ordinance.

B. **The Housing Inspection as a Technique for Improving Housing Quality**

   The inspection procedure should be considered a technique, which used in concert with other techniques, is intended to improve continually the housing quality throughout the community. The inspection procedure, if properly used, is an effective tool in achieving code compliance.

   1. It provides a reasonably accurate measurement of actual dwelling and premises conditions to indicate improvement or slippage in housing quality when compared with previously collected data.

   2. It provides a convenient opportunity for consultation to take place between the occupant and the inspector regarding conditions that do not meet code requirements.

   3. It provides a means of measuring the effectiveness of techniques, such as use of press, radio, TV, and neighborhood improvement projects, which may also be employed to help improve community housing quality.

   4. It provides information that can be later used if some form of legal action becomes necessary to bring about code compliance.

Legal action, as a form of persuasiveness, is often considered to be the least desirable. It can cause adverse publicity for the agency that can hinder its future work. It is costly. Legal action can cause a false impression to be formed by the public regarding the purposes of the agency and the functions of its personnel. It is a last-resort effort that is in a sense an admission of failure at being able to teach housing hygiene principles and persuade their acceptance.

C. The Community Housing Improvement Program

The success of a community housing improvement program generally depends upon several basic factors.

1. Adoption, by municipal officials, of a housing ordinance with realistic code provisions that will help maintain the quality of "good" housing and substantially improve the quality of "poor" housing conditions.
2. The code administration compliance program must be well planned and conducted in a systematic fashion.
3. The program must have sufficient financial support for an adequate number of personnel and other administrative needs.
4. Legal counsel and direct legal aid must be readily available to the program staff when needed.
5. Housing inspectors must be adequately trained and supervised so that they can conduct their work competently.
6. The general acceptance, support, and participation of the public in the housing improvement efforts of the program must be secured.

In the end, this last item will largely determine the measure of success or failure of the program.

The housing agency, as all other governmental units, is a tax-supported public agency that belongs to the people it serves. In the final analysis its future existence to continue serving the needs of the people will depend upon the people's wish to maintain it. This in turn depends upon their understanding of and satisfaction with the services of the agency and the performance of its personnel. Modern thinking is along the line of doing "with" people rather than "for or to" them. When applied to a housing agency and the public it serves, the word "with" implies everything that contributes to good human relations.

II. Human Relations and Attainment of Housing Goals

The term "human relations" as used here actually refers to two types of relationships between people: The personal one-to-one or person-to-person relationship and the relationship that exists between the agency and the general public.

They are interrelated. The public is composed of individuals with attitudes and feelings that when taken jointly make up the public sentiment. This sentiment forms the basis for the relationship that develops between the housing agency and the general public.

A The Housing Inspector and Public Relations

The housing inspector is more concerned with the one-to-one or person-to-person relationships than with the relationship between the agency and the public. The latter is more a responsibility of the supervisory or executive levels of the agency; the housing inspector, however, meets individual members of the public personally on a daily basis. What he does and how he does it, even what he does not do but should do, help to shape the individual's attitudes about the inspector as well as about the agency he represents. Individual attitudes added together form the basis of the public's opinion of the agency and are important in determining whether the public will or will not cooperate with the housing improvement efforts.

The effects of the housing inspector's contacts with the public can have even deeper implications. Since the only contact many members of the public may have with the municipal government is through the housing inspector, he may, to them, represent the municipal administration. This is especially true for the inner-city poverty area resident to whom the housing inspector may well be the municipal government. The housing inspector has more personal contact with members of the public than any other municipal employee, even the mayor. To a large degree, the success of his relationships may well determine the success or failure of many municipal programs other than the housing improvement program.

B **Anatomy of the Person -To - Person Communication Interaction**

Since the person-to-person relationships of the housing inspector have such far-reaching effects, it is important for him to have some idea of what takes place when two persons confront each other in an attempt to communicate.

When two persons meet and attempt to communicate with each other, their reactions to what is said by the other are dependent upon many factors. The behavior of an individual (John) in the presence of another person (Frank) is, at the same time, both a response and a stimulus to the actions of Frank. Because John knows that Frank will react to the manner in which John conducts himself, he (John) is likely to temper his behavior. John may, knowingly or unknowingly to himself, behave in such a way as to bring about certain responses from Frank. John's subsequent behavior thence depends upon whether or not he brings about the desired responses from Frank.

Of course this is an oversimplified explanation of a very complex matter explained in terms of stimulus and response, action and reaction. Under ordinary circumstances, the behavior of persons in interaction flows quite smoothly. This occurs if each party to the interaction has learned to anticipate the response that an action on his part will elicit, as well as to anticipate the responses he will make toward the actions of the other party. *Such interactions flow smoothly, however, only when both parties share the same definitions of their own and each other's acts, as well as an understanding of their relation with each other.*

On the assumption that the housing inspector understands his job to be that of teacher and motivator in addition to that of code enforcement officer, it is to his advantage to have a workable knowledge of the person-to-person communications technique. Armed with this advantage, his job of making people interested in the things they may not want to be interested in becomes easier.

C **How To Interest People In Things They Don't Want To Know**

Every normal human being is interested in many things. Certainly he is interested in himself, his family, and conditions that affect his daily life. To establish an effective communications link the housing inspector must fmd a way to relate what he wants to say with what the other person is already interested in. If he can do this, the inspector can reach him and teach him what he needs to know to improve his housing conditions. This is a two-step process; the inspector must:

- ☑ get the attention or interest of the subject;
- ☑ then do the teaching.

Everyone the inspector tries to reach will have some interest, some need, some desire, to which he can relate himself and his message. At the start, it must be something in which the subject is interested, not something in which the inspector is interested. He must find this need or desire and use it to anchor an emotional or intellectual bridge between himself and his subject. Then he can send his messages across tltis bridge to his subject.

I How To Get The Interest Of The Subject

Obviously, until the inspector has figured out what need or desire he can serve in the subject - and until he states convincingly to the subject - he cannot begin to interest the subject in anything. In fact, the person may not even know that he should have a particular need or desire. This may be especially true with dwellers of inner-city poverty areas who have lived in poor housing conditions so long that their sensibilities to react to these conditions have been dulled. In this instance the best starting place might be to reawaken these sensibilities.

To recognize the needs and desires of the subject, one must know as much about the subject as the subject knows himself - perhaps even more. To do this effectively, the inspector must first recognize and accept certain basic facts:

a. That there is no such thing as "one" or "the" public. All communities - and neighborhoods - have population subgroups based on religion, economic or social status, race, education, nationality, age, sex, and occupation.

b. Childhood rearing patterns vary in each of these subgroups so that the experiences, attitudes, and behavior of individuals belonging to each of these subgroups will be different. These differences may be evident in their attitude and behavior toward the municipal government, its representatives, and even members of other subgroups. Municipal officials the~selves constitute a subgroup that is further broken down by smaller sub groupings formed on the basis of rank, status, or the type of duties performed.

c. Inner-city dwellers in particular may confuse the housing inspector if he is unfamiliar with their problems.

Many of these residents have migrated from remote rural areas that kept them isolated from the mainstream of technological change that has occurred so rapidly in this country. They may have received little or no education or job training. Many came to the city with the sincere hope of improving their condition and becoming a member of the American society. Being unfamiliar with city ways, however, they soon found themselves in difficulty with the law, without a job, and in living conditions that were worse than those they had left in the rural hinterlands.

Often many do not recognize an illness, much less know where to get treatment, even though a health clinic may be just down the street. Some have never been trained to perform simple technical functions such as how to use a washing machine. To survive, many fathers have had temporarily to leave their families in search of work in other cities. Some never return, leaving the women to raise the family. Boys and young men grow up with deeprooted feelings of insecurity, never having had the model of their father to guide their development into manhood. Often any municipal employee represents the real or imagined oppression of the government and is a likely target on which to vent pent-up anxieties.

d. The housing inspector must realize that he also belongs to one or more population subgroups with attitudes and behavior patterns that are different from those found in other groups. As a housing inspector, he must neutralize the attitudes or behavior patterns that may evoke an undesired response from the subject. He must further make it· clear to the person with whom he is trying to establish a communications link that, although there are differences between them, he is unbiased and nonjudgmental in their relationship, and that he expects the same from the subject. These are generally expected characteristics of persons belonging to the subgroupings of municipal officials.

e. By using whatever background knowledge he can learn about the people with whom he must work, the inspector, with some tactful probing, should be able to determine their needs and desires and build a communications bridge to them by establishing a genuine interest in *them*.

2 How To Get Your Message Across

Once the communications bridge has been built, the housing inspector can begin sending messages across. The message he has to tell must be important to the subject, related to some basic need or desire of his, and related in his terms, not the inspector's.

Then he can hope to move the subject in the direction he wants him to go, that is, toward improving his housing conditions.

Every communication has three elements, each of which determines the value of the other two. There is the content of the message, what it is the inspector wants to say. There is the form of the message, how the content is expressed and transmitted, and this includes both the medium and words used. And there is the subject of the communications, the person to whom it is directed.

Obviously until all three of these content, form, and subject are carefully and successfully related to each other, the communication is not likely to have the desired result. The content must be properly and precisely related to the subject. How the message is stated must be properly and precisely related to the content and the subject of the communication. If these three are not effectively related, the intended message will fall short of communicating.

Finally, the communicator, that is, the inspector, must not be message oriented. Although his message may be important to the subject, it may also be new and different, and the importance of the message may have no impact on the subject. The inspector must be always conscious of whom he is trying to reach, of how that person thinks and feels; as he directs his efforts, he shapes his message and form of delivery, as best he can, to fit the subject. To do this, he must start with his subject in mind; that is where persuasive person-to-person communication starts.

D Interagency Relations

The housing inspector should realize that the housing improvement program is only one of manyprograms of municipal administration. During a normal work day, the housing inspector is likely to meet other municipal employees in the same neighborhoods working with the same people.

With the multiplicity of community and personal improvement programs in effect today, especially in inner-city poverty areas, the traffic of public employees can become bewildering, if not irritating, to the neighborhood residents. Naturally, all employees feel their work is important, and in their striving to achieve their goals, compete with other employees for the time, interest, and support of community residents. If competition for the attention of neighborhood residents becomes too intense, the result might well be the polarization of indi viduals around one or a few program activities — those that interest or benefit them mosL Or worse, the result might be sheer apathy and loss of support or interest in any program's efforts. Several things can be done to avert this very undesirable situation and make the efforts of all public employees mutually beneficial. They include the following:

1. The housing inspector should try to determine which employees have duties related to his or perform similar activities. These will usually be health, building, electrical, fire, and various public works employees. He should then try to learn as much as possible about the other employee's work that relates to his own. Then, if he discovers conditions that should be brought to the attention of other departments, he will know enough to determine whether the condition really does constitute a hazard or a violation of another ordinance. Unnecessary inspections can become costly to the municipal administration, time consuming and bothersome for the other employees as well as for the resident.

   A possible result of this type of needless activity can easily result in alienation of both the other city employees and the resident. Eventually the housing inspector will find himself without the participation and support of others in his program efforts.

2. The housing inspector should try to develop lines of liaison or channels of communications with employees of other units. Then, through these channels he should attempt either formally or informally to coordinate the planning and execution of his activities. For example, an occupant of a dwelling would rather have the housing and other necessary inspections done at the same time or on the same day rather than arrange separate appointments on different days.

3. Exchange information and views about the neighborhood and its residents. Keep it general and related only to topics that will directly help improve communications with the residents or otherwise help achieve the desired objectives. All persons regardless of their station in life have the right of freedom from invasion of privacy. The details of a person's life or living circumstances that the inspector may learn during his work should not be idly discussed.

   Perhaps the most important fact the inspector should keep in mind, regarding good interagency relations, is that, although his interest is primarily focused on one program area, he is part of a larger team working together to improve the conditions of the total community.

BUILDING ASPECTS OF A HOUSING INSPECTION

CONTENTS

		Page
I.	Background Factors	1
II.	Housing Construction Terminology	1
III.	Structure	4
IV.	Discussion of Inspection Techniques	15
V.	Noise as an Environmental Stress	17

BUILDING ASPECTS OF A HOUSING INSPECTION

The principle function of a house is to furnish protection from the elements. In its current stage, however, our civilization requires that a home provide not only shelter but also privacy, safety, and reasonable protection of our physical and mental health. A living facility that fails to offer these essentials through adequately designed and properly maintained interiors and exteriors cannot be termed "healthful housing."

I. Background Factors

In this chapter, a building will be considered in terms of its major components: heating, plumbing, and electrical systems. Each of these items will be examined in detail in future chapters. Attention will be given in this chapter to the portions of a building not visible upon completion of the ceiling, roof, and interior and exterior walls in order to give the reader an understanding of generally accepted construction practices. Emphasis, however, will be placed upon the visible interior and exterior parts of a completed dwelling that have a bearing on the soundness, state of repair, and safety of the dwelling both during intended use and in the event of a fire. These are some of the elements that the housing inspector must examine when making a thorough housing inspection.

II. Housing Construction Terminology

(Key to Component Parts Numbered in Figure 1)

A Fireplace

1 **Chimney** - A vertical masonry shaft of reinforced concrete or other approved non-combustible, heat resisting material enclosing one or more flues. It removes the products of combustion from solid, liquid, or gaseous fuel.

2 **Flue Liner** - The flue is the hole in the chimney. The liner, usually of terra cotta, protects the brick from harmful smoke gases.

3 **Chimney Cap** - This top is generally of concrete. It protects the brick from weather.

4 **Chimney Flashing** - Sheet-metal flashing provides a tight joint between chimney and roof.

5 **Firebrick** - An ordinary brick cannot withstand the heat of direct fire, and so special firebrick is used to line the fireplace.

6 **Ash Dump** - A trap door to let the ashes drop to a pit below, from where they may be easily removed.

7 **Cleanout Door** - The door to the ash pit or the bottom of a chimney through which the chimney can be cleaned.

8 **Chimney Breast** - The inside face or front of a fireplace chimney.

9 **Hearth** - The floor of a fireplace that extends into the room for safety purposes.

B Roof

10 **Ridge** - The top intersection of two opposite adjoining roof surfaces.

11 **Ridge Board** - The board that follows along under the ridge.

12 **Roof Rafters** - The structural members that support the roof.

13 **Collar Beam** - Really not a beam at all. A tie that keeps the roof from spreading. Connects similar rafters on opposite side of roof.

14 **Roof Insulation** - An insulating material (usually rock wool or fiberglas) in a blanket form placed between the roof rafters for the purpose of keeping a house warm in the winter, cool in the summer.

15 **Roof Sheathing** - The boards that provide the base for the finished roof.

Figure 1. Housing Construction Terminology

16 **Roofing** - The wood, asphalt, or asbestos shingles - or tile, slate or metal - that form the outer protection against the weather.

17 **Cornice** - A decorative element made up of molded members usually placed at or near the top of an exterior or interior wall.

18 **Gutter** - The trough that gathers rainwater from a roof.

19 **Downspouts** - The pipe that leads the water down from the gutter.

20 **Storm Sewer Tile** - The underground pipe that receives the water from the downspouts and carries it to the sewer.

21 **Gable** - The triangular end of a building with a sloping roof.

22 **Barage Board** - The fascia or board at the gable just under the edge of the roof.

23 **Louvers** - A series of slanted slots arranged to keep out rain, yet allow ventilation.

C Walls and Floors

24 **Corner Post** - The vertical member at the corner of the frame, made up to receive inner and outer covering materials.

25 **Studs** - The vertical wood members of the house, usually 2 X 4's generally spaced every 16 inches.

26 **Sill** - The board that is laid first on the foundation, and on which the frame rests.

27 **Plate** - The board laid across the top ends of the studs to hold them even and rigid.

28 **Corner Bracing** - Diagonal strips to keep the frame square and plumb.

29 **Sheathing** - The first layer of outer wall covering nailed to the studs.

30 **Joist** - The structural members or beams that hold up the floor or ceiling, usually 2 X 10's or 2 X 12's spaced 16 inches apart.

31 **Bridging** - Cross bridging or solid. Members at the middle or third points of joist spans to brace one to the next and to prevent their twisting.

32 **Subflooring** - The rough boards that are laid over the joist. Usually laid diagonally.

33 **Flooring Paper** - A felt paper laid on the rough floor to stop air infiltration and, to some extent, noise.

34 **Finish Flooring** - Usually hardwood, of tongued and grooved strips.

35 **Building Paper** - Paper placed outside the sheathing, not as a vapor barrier, but to prevent water and air from leaking in. Building paper is also used as a tarred felt under shingles or siding to keep out moisture or wind.

36 **Beveled Siding** - Sometimes called clapboards, with a thick butt and a thin upper edge lapped to shed water.

37 **Wall Insulation** - A blanket of wool or reflective foil placed inside the walls.

38 **Metal Lath** - A mesh made from sheet metal onto which plaster is applied.

D **Foundation and Basement**

39 **Finished Grade Line** - The top of the ground at the foundation.

40 **Foundation Wall** - The wall of poured concrete (shown) or concrete blocks that rests on the footing and supports the remainder of the house.

41 **Termite Shield** - A metal baffle to prevent termites from entering the frame.

42 **Footing** - The concrete pad that carries the entire weight of the house upon the earth.

43 **Footing Drain Tile** - A pipe with cracks at the joints to allow underground water to drain in and away before it gets into the basement.

44 **Basement Floor Slab** - The 4- or 5-inch layer of concrete that forms the basement floor.

45 **Gravel Fill** - Placed under the slab to allow drainage and to guard against a damp floor.

46 **Girder** - A main beam upon which floor joists rest. Usually of steel, but also of wood.

47 **Backfill** - Earth, once dug out, that has been replaced and tamped down around the foundation.

48 **Areaway** - An open space to allow light and air to a window. Also called a light well.

49 **Area Wall** - The wall, of metal or concrete, that forms the open area.

E **Windows and Doors**

50 **Window** - An opening in a building for admitting light and air. It usually has a pane or panes of glass and is set in a frame or sash that is generally movable for opening and shutting.

51 **Window Frame** - The lining of the window opening.

52   **Window Sash** - The inner frame, usually movable, that holds the glass.

53   **Lintel** - The structural beam over a window or door opening.

54   **Window Casing** - The decorative strips surrounding a window opening on the inside.

F   Stairs and Entry

55   **Entrance Canopy** - A roof extending over the entrance door.

56   **Furring** - Falsework or framework necessary to bring the outer surface to where we want it.

57   **Stair Tread** - The horizontal strip where we put our foot when we climb up or down the stairs.

58   **Stair Riser** - The vertical board connecting one tread to the next.

59   **Stair Stringer** - The sloping board that supports the ends of the steps.

60   **Newel** - The post that terminates the railing.

61   **Stair Rail** - The bar used for a handhold when we use the stairs.

62   **Balusters** - Vertical rods or spindles supporting a rail.

III. Structure

A   Foundation

The word **foundation** is used to mean:
1. Construction below grade such as footings, cellar or basement walls.
2. The composition of the earth on which the building rests.
3. Special construction such as pilings and piers used to support the building.

The foundation bed may be composed of solid rock, sand, gravel, or unconsolidated sand or clay. Rock, sand, or gravel are the most reliable foundation materials. Unconsolidated sand and clay, though found in many sections of the country, are not as desirable, because they are subject to sliding and settling.

The footing (see Figure 2) distributes the weight of the building over a sufficient area of ground so as to ensure that the foundation walls will stand properly. Footings are usually constructed of a masonry-type material such as concrete; however, in the past wood and stone have been used. Some older houses have been constructed without footings.

Although it is usually difficult to determine the condition of a footing without excavating the foundation, a footing in a state of disrepair or lack of a footing will usually be indicated either by large

Figure 2. Foundation Details
SECTION-EXTERIOR WALL WITH EXCAVATED CELLAR

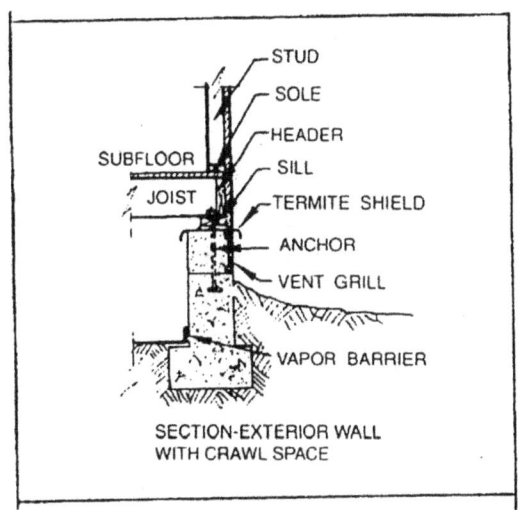

Section - Exterior Wall with Crawl Space

Section - Slab on Grade - Porch

cracks or by settlement in the foundation walls (see Figure 3).

Foundation wall cracks are usually diagonal, starting from the top, the bottom; or the end of the wall. Cracks that do not extend to at least one edge of the wall may not be caused by foundation problems. Such wall cracks may be due to other structural problems and should also be reported.

The foundation walls support the weight of the structure and transfer this weight to the footings. The foundation walls may be made of stone, brick, concrete, or concrete blocks and should be moisture proofed with either a membrane of water-proof material or a coating of portland cement mortar. The membrane may consist of plastic sheeting or a sandwich of standard roofing felt joined and covered with tar or asphalt. The purpose of waterproofing the foundation walls is to prevent water from penetrating the wall material and leaving the basement or cellar walls damp.

Holes in the foundation walls are a common finding in many old houses. These holes may be caused by missing bricks or blocks. Holes and cracks in a foundation wall are undesirable because they make a convenient entry for rats and other rodents and also indicate the possibility of further structural deterioration. These holes should not be confused with adequately installed vents in the foundation wall that permit ventilation and prevent moisture entrapment.

The basement or cellar floor should be made of concrete placed on at least 6 inches of gravel. The purpose of a concrete floor is to protect the basement or cellar from invasion by rodents or from flooding. The gravel distributes ground water movements under the concrete floor, reducing the possibility of the water's penetrating the floor. A waterproof membrane, such as plastic sheeting, should be laid before the concrete is placed for additional protection against flooding.

The basement or cellar floor should be gradually but uniformly sloped towards a drain or a series of drains from all directions. These drains permit the basement or cellar floor to be drained if it becomes flooded.

Evidence of ineffective waterproofing or moisture proofing will be indicated by water or moisture marks on the floor and walls.

Figure 3. Foundation Cracks

CRACKS IN THE MASONRY FOUNDATION WALL ALONG THE MASONRY JOINTS.

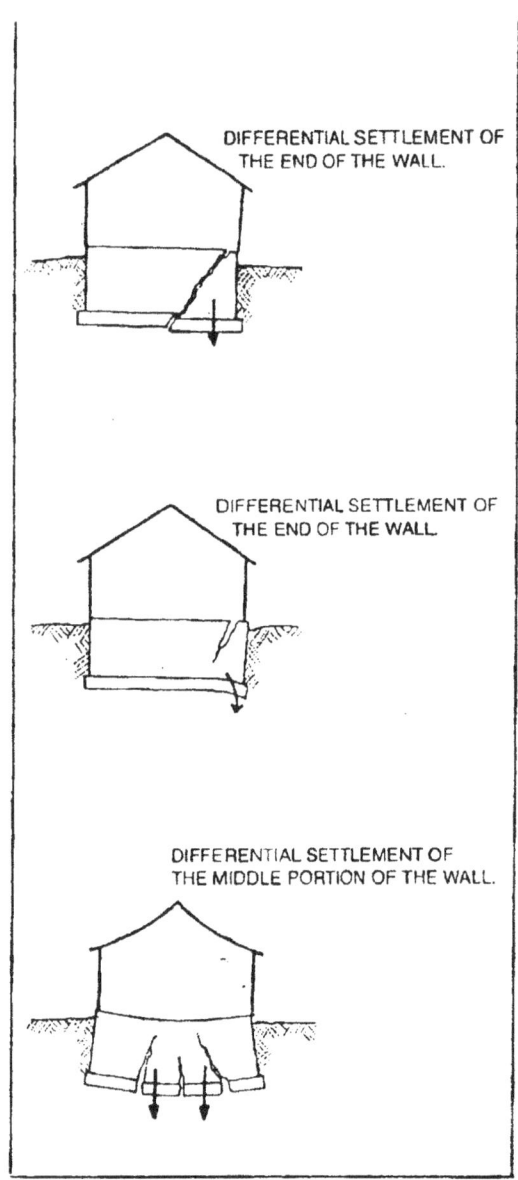

DIFFERENTIAL SETTLEMENT OF THE END OF THE WALL.

DIFFERENTIAL SETTLEMENT OF THE END OF THE WALL.

DIFFERENTIAL SETTLEMENT OF THE MIDDLE PORTION OF THE WALL.

Cellar doors, hatchways, and basement windows should be weathertight and rodent proof. A hatchway can be inspected by standing at the lower portion with the doors closed; if daylight can be seen, the door probably needs repair.

B **Framing**

Many different types of house-framing systems are found in various sections of the country; however, the majority of the members in each framing system are the same. They include:

1 **Foundation Sills:** (see Figure 4 and 5). The purpose of the sill is to provide support or a bearing surface for the outside walls of the building. The sill is the first part of the frame to be placed and rests directly on the foundation wall. It is bolted to the foundation wall by sill anchors. It is good practice to protect the sill against termites by extending the foundation wall to at least 18 inches above the ground and using a non-corroding metal shield continuously around the outside top of the foundation wall.

2 **Flooring Systems:** (see Figure 5). The flooring system is composed of a combination of girders, joists, sub-flooring, and finished flooring that may be made up of concrete, steel, or wood. Joists are laid perpendicular to the girders, at about 16 inches on centers, and are the members to which the sub-flooring is attached. When the subfloor is wood, it may be nailed at either right angles or diagonally to the joists.

As shown in Figure 5, a girder is a member that in certain framing systems supports the joists and is usually a larger section than the joists it supports. Girders are found in framing systems where there are no interior bearing walls or where the span between bearing walls is greater than the joists are capable of spanning. The most common application of a girder is to support the first floor in residences. Often a board known as a ledger is applied to the side of a wood girder or beam to form a ledge for the joists to rest upon. The girder, in turn, is supported by wood posts or steel "lally columns" which extend from the cellar or basement floor to the girder.

3 **Studs:** (see Figure 4 and 5). Wall studs are almost always 2 by 4

inches; studs 2 by 6 inches are occasionally used to provide a wall thick enough to permit the passage of waste pipes. There are two types of walls or partitions: bearing and non-bearing. A bearing wall is constructed at right angles to and supports the joists. A nonbearing wall or partition acts as a screen or enclosure; hence, the headers in it are often parallel to the joists of the floor above.

In general, studs like joists are spaced 16 inches on center. In light construction such as garages and summer cottages where plaster is omitted, or some other material is used for a wall finish, wider spacing on studs is common.

Openings for windows or doors must be framed in studs. This framing consists of horizontal members called "headers," and vertical members called "trimmers" (see Figure 1).

Since the vertical spaces between studs can act as flues to transmit flames in the event of a fire, "fire stops" are important in preventing or retarding fire from spreading through a building by way of air passages in walls, floors, and partitions. Fire stops are wood obstructions placed between studs or floor joists to prevent fire from spreading in these natural fluespaces.

4 **Interior Wall Finish:** Many types of materials are used for covering interior walls and ceilings, but the principal types are plaster and dry-wall construction. Plaster is a mixture, usually lime, sand, and water, applied in two or three coats to lath to form a hard-wall surface. Dry-wall finish is a material that requires little, if any, water for application. More specifically, dry-wall finish may be gypsum board, plywood, fiberboard, or wood in various sizes and forms.

Figure 4. Wall Framing

SECTION-JOISTS AT RIGHT ANGLES TO EXTERIOR WALL WITH CRAWL SPACE

Figure 5. Floor Construction

Gypsum board is a sheet material composed of a gypsum filler faced with paper. Sheets are usually 4 feet wide and can be obtained in lengths up to 12 feet. In dry-wall construction, gypsum boards are fastened to the studs either vertically or horizontally and then painted. The edges along the length of the sheet are recessed to receive joint cement and tape.

A plaster finish requires a base upon which plaster can be spread. Wood lath at one time was the plaster base most commonly used, but today gypsum-board lath is more popular. It has paper faces with a gypsum filler. Such lath is 16 by 48 inches and 1/2 or 3/8 inches thick.

It is applied horizontally across the studs. Gypsum lath may be perforated to improve the bond and thus lengthen the time the plaster can remain intact when exposed to fire. The building codes in some cities require that gypsum lath be perforated. Expanded-metal lath may also be used as a plaster base. Expanded-metal lath consists of sheet metal slit and expanded to form openings to hold the plaster. Metal lath is usually 27 by 96 inches and is fastened to the studs.

Plaster is applied over the base to a minimum thickness of 1/2 inch. Because some drying may take place in wood-framing members after the house is completed, some shrinkage can be expected, which, in turn, may cause plaster cracks to develop around openings and in corners. Strips of lath imbedded in the plaster at these locations prevent cracks.

On the inside face of studs that form an exterior wall, vapor barriers are used to prevent condensation on the wall. The vapor barrier is an asphalted paper or metal foil through which moisture-laden air cannot travel.

5 **Stairways:** (see Figure 6). The general purpose of the standards for stairway dimensions is to ensure that there is adequate headroom, width, and uniformity in riser and tread size of every step to accommodate the expected traffic on each stairway safely.

Interior stairways should be not less than 44 inches in width. The width of a stairway may be reduced to 36 inches in one- and two-family dwellings. Stairs with closed risers should have maximum risers of 8 1/4 inches and a minimum tread of 9 inches plus 1 1/4-inch nosing. Basement stairs are often constructed with open risers. These stairs should have maximum risers of 8 1/4 inches and minimum treads of 9 inches plus 1/2-inch nosing. The headroom in all parts of the stair enclosure should be no less than 80 inches.

Exterior stairway dimensions should be the same as those called for in interior stairways, except that the headroom requirement does not apply.

6 **Windows:** The four general classifications of windows for residences are:

a Double-hung sash window that moves up or down, balanced by weights hung on chains or ropes, or springs on each side.

b Casement window sash is hinged at the side and can be hung so that it will swing outward or inward.

c Awning window - usually has two or more glass panes that are hinged at the top and swing about a horizontal axis.

d Sliding window - usually has two or more glass panes that slide past one another on a horizontal track.

The principal parts of a double-hung window (see Figure 4-7) are the lights, the top rail-framing members, bars or muntins that separate the lights, stiles - side-framing members, bottom rail, sash weights, and sash cords or chains. (All rails are horizontal, all stiles vertical.) The casement window's principal parts include: top and bottom rails, muntins, butt hinges, and jamb. All types of windows should open freely and close securely.

The exterior sill is the bottom projection of a window. The drip cap is a separate piece of wood projecting over the top of the window and is a component of the window casing.

Figure 7. Window Details

7 **Doors**: There are many styles of doors both for exterior and interior use. Interior doors should offer a rea-

sonable degree of privacy. Exterior doors must, in addition to offering privacy, protect the interior of the structure from the elements. The various parts of a door have the same definitions as the corresponding parts of a window.

The most common types of doors are:

a **Batten door**: This consists of boards nailed together in various ways. The simplest is two layers nailed to each other at right angles, usually with each layer at 45 degrees to the vertical.

Another type of batten door consists of vertical boards nailed at right angles to several (two to four) cross strips called ledgers, with diagonal bracing members nailed between ledgers. If vertical members corresponding to ledgers are added at the sides, the verticals are called frames.

Batten doors are often found in cellars and other places where appearance is not a factor and economy is desired.

b **Flush doors**: Solid flush doors are perfectly flat, usually on both sides, although occasionally they are made flush on one side and paneled on the other. Flush doors sometimes are solid planking, but they are commonly veneered and possess a core of small pieces of white pine or other wood. These pieces are glued together with staggered end joints. Along the sides, top, and bottom are glued 3/4-inch edge strips of the same wood, used to create a smooth surface that can be cut or planed. The front and back faces are then covered with a 1/8-to 1/4-inch layer of veneer.

Solid flush doors may be used on both the interior and exterior.

c **Hollow-core doors**: These, like solid flush doors, are perfectly flat, but unlike solid doors, the core consists mainly of a grid of crossed wooden slats or some other type of grid construction. Faces are 3-ply plywood instead of one or two plies of veneer, and the surface veneer may be any species of wood, usually hardwood. The edges of the core are solid wood and are made wide enough at the appropriate places to accommodate locks and butts. Doors of this kind are considerably lighter than solid flush doors.

Hollow-core doors are usually used as interior doors.

d **Paneled doors**: Most doors are paneled, with most panels consisting of solid wood or plywood, either "raised" or "flat," although exterior doors frequently have one or more panels of glass, in which case they are called "lights." One or more panels may be employed although the number seldom exceeds eight. Paneled doors may be used both on the interior or exterior.

In addition to the various types of wood doors, metal is often used as a veneer or for the frame.

In general, the horizontal members are called rails and the vertical members are called stiles. Every door has a top and bottom rail, and some may have intermediate rails. There are always at least two stiles, one on each side of the door. The frame of a doorway is the portion to which the door is hinged. It consists of two side jambs and a head jamb, with an integral or attached stop against which the door closes.

Exterior door frames are ordinarily of softwood plank, with side rabbitted to receive the door in the same way as casement windows. At the foot is a sill, made of hardwood to withstand the wear of traffic, and sloped down and out to shed water.

Interior door frames are similar to exterior, except that they are often set directly on the hardwood flooring without a sill.

Building codes throughout the country call for doors in various locations within the structure to be fire resistant. These doors are often covered with metal or some other fire-resistant materials, and some are completely constructed of metal. Fire-resistant doors are usually located between a garage and a house, stairwells and hallways, all boiler rooms. The fire resistance rating required for various doors differs with local fire codes

C **Roof Framing** (see Figures 1, 4, 8, and 9)

Rafters serve the same purpose for the roof as joists do for floors, i.e., providing support for sheathing and roofing material. Rafters are usually spaced 20 inches on center.

1 **Collar Beam:** Collar beams are ties between rafters on opposite sides of the roof. If the attic is to be used for rooms, the collar beam may double as the ceiling joist.

2 **Purlin:** A purlin is the horizontal member that forms the support for the rafters at the intersection of the two slopes of a gambrel roof.

3 **Ridge Board:** A ridge board is a horizontal member against which the rafters rest at their upper ends; it forms a lateral tie to make them secure.

4 **Hip:** Like a ridge except that it slopes. The intersection of two adjacent, rather than two opposite, roof planes.

5 **Roof Boards:** The manner in which roof boards are applied depends upon the type of roofing material. Roof boards may vary from tongue-and-groove lumber to plywood panels.

6 **Dormer:** The term dormer window is applied to all windows in the roof of a building, whatever their size and shape.

D **Exterior Walls and Trim** (see Figure 4 and 9)

Exterior walls are enclosure walls whose purpose is to make the building weather-tight. In most one- to three-story buildings they also serve as bearing walls. These walls may be made of many different materials.

Frequently used framed exterior walls appear to be of brick construction. In this situation, the brick is only one course thick and is called a brick veneer. It supports nothing but itself and is kept from toppling by ties connected to the frame wall.

In frame construction the base material of the exterior walls is called "sheathing." The sheathing material may be square-edge, shiplap, or tongue-and-groove boards.

In recent construction there has been a strong trend toward the use of plywood or composition panels.

Figure 8. Cornice Construction

Figure 9. Cornice Construction

Sheathing, in addition to serving as a base course for the finished siding material, stiffens the frame to resist sway caused by wind. It is for this reason that sheathing has been applied diagonally on frame buildings.

The finished siding may be clapboard, shingles, aluminum, brick asphalt, wood, and so forth, or a combination thereof. Good aluminum siding has a backer board that serves as added insulation and affords rigidity to the siding. Projecting cornices are a decorative trim found at the top of the building's roofline. A parapet wall is that part of the masonry wall that extends up and beyond the roofline and is capped with a noncombustible material. It helps prevent spread of fire, provides a rest for fire department ladders, and helps prevent people on the roof from falling off.

Many types of siding, shingles, and other exterior coverings are applied over the sheathing. Wood siding, cedar, and other wood shingles or shakes, clapboard, common siding (called bevel siding), composition siding, asbestos, cement shingles, asbestos-cement siding, and the aforementioned aluminum siding are commonly used for exterior coverings. Clapboards and common siding differ only in the length of the pieces. Clapboards are 4 feet long while panel siding comes in lengths from 6 to 16 feet. Composition siding is made of felt and asphalt, which are often shaped to look like brick. Asbestos and cement shingles are rigid and produce a covering that is fire resistant. Cedar wood shingles are also manufactured with a backer board that gives insulation and fire-resistant qualities. Asbestos cement siding made of asbestos fiber and portland cement has good fire-resistant qualities and is a rigid covering.

E Roof Coverings (Flexible Material Class)

1 **Asphalt Shingle:** The principal damage to asphalt shingle roofs is caused by the action of strong winds on shingles nailed too high. Usually the shingles affected by winds are those in the four or five courses nearest the ridge and in the area

extending about 5 feet down from the edge or rake of the roof.

2. **Asphalt Built-up Roofs:** These may be un-surfaced, the coating of bitumen being exposed directly to the weather, or they may be surfaced having slag or gravel imbedded in the bituminous coating. The use of surfacing material is desirable as a protection against wind damage and the elements. This type of roof should have enough pitch to drain water readily.

3. **Coal Tar Pitch Built-up Roofs:** This type roof must be surfaced with slag or gravel. Coal tar pitch built-up roof should always be used on deck pitched less than 1/2 inch per foot; that is, where waler may collect and stand. This type roof should be inspected on completion, 6 months later, and then at least once a year, preferably in the fall. When the top coating of bitumen shows damage or has become badly weathered, it should be renewed (rigid material class).

4. **Slate Roofs:** The most common problem with slate roofs is the replacement of broken slates. Roofs of this type normally render long service with little or no repair.

5. **Tile Roofs:** Replacement of broken shingle tiles is the main maintenance problem. This is one of the most expensive roofing materials. It requires very little maintenance and gives long service.

6. **Copper Roofs:** Usually are of 16-ounce copper sheeting and applied to permanent structures. When properly installed, they require practically no maintenance or repair. Proper installation allows for expansion and contraction with changes in temperature.

7. **Galvanized Iron Roofs:** Maintenance is done principally by removing rust and keeping roof well painted. Leaks can be corrected by re-nailing, caulking, or replacing all or part of the sheet or sheets in disrepair.

8. **Wood Shingle Roofs:** The most important factors of this type roof are its pitch and exposure, the character of wood, kind of nails used, and preservative treatment given shingles. Creosote and coal tar preservative are satisfactory for both treated and untreated shingles.

9. **Flashing:** Valleys in roofs that are formed by the junction of two downward slopes may be finished, open, or closed. In a closed valley the slates, tiles, or shingles of one side meet those of the other, and the flashing below them may be comparatively narrow. In an open valley, the flashing, which may be made of zinc, copper, or aluminum, is laid in a continuous strip, extending 12 to 18 inches on each side of the valley, while the tiles or slates do not come within 4 to 6 inches of it.

The ridges built up on a sloping roof where it runs down against a vertical projection, like a chimney or a skylight, should be weather-proofed with flashing.

Metal flashings are generally used with slate, tile, metal, and wood shingles. Failure of roof flashing is usually due to exposed nails that have come loose. The loose nails allow the flashing to lift with leakage resulting.

10. **Gutters and Leaders:** Gutters and leaders should be of noncombustible materials. They should be securely fastened to the structure and spill into a storm sewer if the neighborhood is so provided. When there is no storm sewer, a concrete or stone block placed on the ground beneath the leader prevents water from eroding the lawn. This store

block is called a splash block. Gutters will not become plugged if protected against clogging of leaves and twigs. Gutters should be checked every spring and fall and then cleaned out when necessary.

IV. Discussion of Inspection Techniques

A serious building defect may often be observed during a housing inspector's routine examination. In many cases it is beyond the scope of the housing inspector's background to analyze the underlying causes and to recommend a course of action that will facilitate repair in an efficient and economical manner. In situations such as this, it is important that the inspector realize his limitations and refer the matter to the proper expert.

A prime example of a technically complex situation that a housing inspector might observe is a leaning, buckling, or bulging foundation or bearing wall. This problem may be the result of a number of hidden or interacting problems. For example, it may be the result of differential building settlement or failure of a structural beam or girder. It is beyond the scope of the housing inspector's responsibilities to discover the cause of the defect, but it is his responsibility to note the problem and refer it to the proper authority. In this case the proper authority would be a building inspector.

In the aforementioned situation where a bulging foundation wall was discovered, this would obviously constitute a violation of the housing ordinance and should be written up as such by the housing inspector. Since the housing inspector is generally not qualified to determine whether the house should be evacuated because it is in danger of imminent collapse, he should seek the advice of a building inspector.

A question that frequently arises is *which violations should be referred to an expert?* Needless to say, circumstances that obviously fall within the jurisdiction of another department should be referred to the department. The housing inspector should discuss with his supervisor any situation in which he feels inadequate to make a decision. In all cases the inspector should inform his supervisor before referring a problem to another agency or expert.

Another reason for referral to other departments is that when a remedial action is completed the other department will be in a better position to determine whether the job is satisfactory.

This principle of referral should be applied to every portion of the inspection, whether it deals with health, heating, plumbing, gas, or electrical as well as structural defects.

Certain structural items should be recognized as unsafe by the housing inspector. For example, a beam that has sagged or slanted may cause a portion of or an entire floor to sag or slope. Where a sagging or sloping floor is found, examine the ceiling of the room below or the basement for a broken or dropped girder or joist.

Doors and windows that are out of level will not close completely. It may be possible to see outside light through openings around window rails and door jambs. If an inspector detects such a situation, the condition of the supporting girders, girts, posts, and studs should be questioned, since this condition is evidence that some of these members may be termite infested or rotted and may be causing the outside wall to sag. Glass panes in doors and windows should be replaced if found to be broken or missing. Windows should also be checked for proper operation, and items such as broken sash cords or chains noted.

If the roof of the structure appears to be sagging, the inspector should make a special effort to examine the rafters, purlin, collar beams, and ridge boards if these members are exposed as in unfinished attics. The condition of the roof boards may be examined while he is in the attic. If light can be seen between these boards the roof is unsound. Evidence of a leaking roof will be indicated by loose plaster or peeling or stained paint and wall paper. Areas of the roof where flashing occurs, such as around the chimney, are frequent origins of roof leaks. It is essential that the leak be found and repaired, not only to prevent the entrance of moisture into the building, but also to prevent the loosening of the plaster, rotting of timbers, and extension of damage to the remainder of the house.

Gutters and rain leaders should be placed around the entire building to insure proper drainage of water. This will lessen the possibility of seepage of water through siding and window frames, and entrance of water into the cellar or basement. Lack of or leaking gutters may result in rotting of the siding or erosion of the exposed portion of the cellar or basement walls. This situation commonly exists where the mortar between bricks or concrete blocks in foundation walls is found to be heavily eroded. Gutters should be free from dirt and leaves.

The exterior siding should be in sound, weathertight condition. Peeled or worn paint on wood siding will expose the bare wood to the elements and result in splitting and warping of siding. This condition will eventually lead to the entrance of rain water with resultant rotting of the sheathing and studs as well as inside dampness and falling plaster. Sound and painted siding will prevent major repairs and expenses in the future. This condition will often be particularly prevalent on the north face of the structure.

Roof and chimneys should be inspected for tilting, missing bricks, deterioration of flashing, and pointing of chimney bricks. In addition, roof covering should be checked for broken spots and missing shingles or tiles. Roof doors should be metal clad, self-closing, tight fitting, and unlockable. The roof should also be examined for weather-tightness and broken TV antennas.

Porches should be carefully examined for weakened treads, missing or cracked boards, holes, and holes covered with tin plates, railing rigidity, missing posts, handrail rigidity, condition of the columns that support the porch roof, and the condition of the porch roof itself. The open section beneath the porch should be inspected for broken lattice-work. Check under the porch for accumulation of dirt and debris that can offer a harborage for vermin and rodents.

Loose plaster and missing or peeling wallpaper or paint should be noted. Bugs and cockroaches eat the paste from the wallpaper while leaving behind loose paper.

The basic parts of a stairway that a housing inspector should be able to identify correctly are the following:

A Riser

B Tread

C Nosing

D Handrail

E Balustrade and Balusters, the Vertical Members that Support the Handrail, and

F The Soffit, Underpart of the Stairway.

In the examination of a stairway (be careful to turn the light on) initially check the underside, if visible, to see if it is intact. Then proceed slowly up the stairs placing full weight on each tread and checking for loose, wobbling, or uneven treads and risers. Regardless of the size of the treads or risers they should all be of uniform size. For all stairs that rise 3 or more feet, a handrail should be present and in a sound and rigid condition.

Any fireplace should conform to the requirements of the local code. An unused fireplace that has its opening covered with wallpaper or other material should have a solid seal behind the paper. Operable fireplaces should have a workable damper and a fire screen, and should be clean.

Garages and accessory structures should be inspected in the same manner as the main building.

Sidewalks and driveways, whether constructed of flagstone, concrete, or asphalt, should be checked for creaking, buckling, and other conditions dangerous to pedestrian travel.

Stone, brick, or concrete steps should be inspected for cracks, deterioration, and pointing.

Fences should be in a sound condition and painted. Fire escapes should be checked for paint condition, loose or broken treads and rails, proper operating condition, and proper connection to the house.

V. Noise as an Environmental Stress

People feel comfortable in an environment with a low-level, soothing, steady, unobstrusive level of sound, typical of the natural undisturbed environment. All of us have experienced the anguish that noise can cause, whether it be noise from a neighbor's television, the grinding of truck gears while asleep, the persistent whine of a fan motor, or the sound of children racing down the halls. These annoyances experienced in the home are producing public demands for noise control legislation.

Not only is noise disturbing, but studies also indicate that extreme noise can cause deafness and perhaps interfere with other bodily functions.

While few existing housing ordinances contain enforceable noise provisions, noise problems must be considered by the building inspector because they intimately affect and are affected by his decisions. As a housing inspector, you can help residents by suggesting corrective noise measures that can be taken; you can refer them to agencies, if needed, for corrective action; you can help them to understand that their noisy environment can place limitations on their behavior, capabilities, and satisfaction with their home.

Noise is unwanted sound. Noise can travel through air or through the building structure. The first stage of noise control is the control of sound at its source. If attempts to quiet the source are not completely successful, then other, more expensive corrective measures will be required.

Although a visual examination of a dwelling may detect some sources of noise leaks (see Figure 10) such as wide gaps or cracks at ceiling, floor, or adjoining wall edges, it is usually inadequate since it fails to detect sources of noise leaks hidden from the eye. A far more effective test is to be alert for the operation of some noisy device like a vacuum cleaner in a closed room and listen near the other side of the wall for any noise leakage. The ear is a reasonably good sensing device. If a noise leak is noticed, the partition may be surveyed at critical points with a bright flashlight while an observer looks for light leakage in a darkened room on the other side. Detection of any light leakage in the darkened room will signify a noise leak.

Noise carried as vibration by a building structure is called structure-borne noise. Detecting structure-borne noise caused by the operation of mechanical equipment is somewhat more difficult (see Figure 11). With noisy equipment in operation, the inspector can sometimes locate noise leaks or structure-borne noise paths by conducting similar hearing tests along with pressing the ear against various room surfaces or using fingertips to sense the vibration of these surfaces.

A Airborne Noise

The sources of airborne noise that cause the most frequent disturbances in the home are audio instruments such as televisions, radios, phonographs, or pianos; adults and children speaking loudly, singing, crying and shouting; household appliances such as garbage disposals, dishwashers, vacuum cleaners, clothes washers, and dryers; plumbing noises such as pipes knocking, toilets flushing, and water running.

The disturbing influences of airborne noise are generally limited to the areas near the noise source. For example, a phonograph may cause annoyance in rooms of a neighbor's apartment adjacent to the phonograph but rarely in rooms farther removed unless doors or passageways are left open. Sound absorption materials such as carpeting, acoustical tile, drapery, and upholstered furniture in the intervening rooms may often provide a significant reduction in the disturbing noise before it reaches rooms where quiet is desired.

Under no conditions should sound-absorptive materials be used on the surfaces of walls and ceilings for the sole purpose of preventing the transmission of sound as structure-borne noise. To do so would be a complete waste of effort. To illustrate, imagine the noise conducted by a wall constructed solely of drapery or acoustical tile attached to studs. The noise level in the room would be reduced, but sound produced in the room would pass through the wall to adjoining rooms with little, if any, reduction in noise level. Sound absorptive materials should be used in and near areas of high noise levels to limit airborne noise at the source of the noise and reduce the effects of noise along corridors.

The transmission of noise from one completely enclosed room to an adjoining room separated by a partition wall may be either direct transmission through the wall, indirect transmission through other walls, ceilings, and floors common to both rooms, or through corridors adjacent to such rooms.

In some older wood frame houses, the open troughs between studs and joists are efficient sound transmission paths. This noise transmission by indirect paths is known as "flanking transmission" (see Figure 10 and 11). In addition to the flanking paths, there may be noise leaks particularly along the ceiling, floor, and sidewall edges of the wall. In order to obtain the highest sound insulation performance, a partition wall must be of airtight construction. Care must be exercised to seal all openings, gaps, holes, joints, and penetrations of piping and conduits with a nonsetting caulking compound. Even hairline cracks, particularly at adjoining wall, floor, and ceiling edges, transmit a substantially greater amount of noise than would normally be expected on the basis of the size of the crack.

Figure 10. Flanking Transmission of Airborne Noise

FLANKING NOISE PATHS	NOISE LEAKS
F1 Open plenums over walls, false ceilings	L1 Poor seal at ceiling edges
F2 Unbaffled duct runs	L2 Poor seal around duct penetrations
F3 Outdoor path, window to window	L3 Poor mortar joints, porous masonry block
F4 Continuous unbaffled inductor Units	L4 Poor seal at sidewall, filler panel, etc.
F5 Hall path, open vents	L5 Back-to-back cabinets, poor workmanship
F6 Hall path, louvered doors	L6 Holes, gaps at wall penetrations
F7 Hall path, openings under doors	L7 Poor seal at floor edges
F8 Open troughs in floor-ceiling structure	L8 Back-to-back electrical outlets
	L9 Holes, gaps at floor penetrations

Other points to consider are these: leaks are (a) batten strip A/O post connections of prefabricated walls, (b) under-floor pipe or service chases, (c) recessed, spanning light fixtures, (d) ceiling and floor cover plates of movable walls, (e) unsupported A/O unbacked wall-board joints (f) edges and backing of built-in cabinets and appliances, (g) prefabricated, hollow metal, exterior curtain walls.

It is often helpful to use one sound to drown out another disturbing noise; for example, music on the radio can be used to drown out the noise of traffic. The use of sound to drown out noise is particularly useful in masking noises that occur infrequently, such as accelerating or braking vehicles, periodic mechanical equipment noise, barking dogs, laughter, or shouting.

B **Structure-Borne Noise**

Structure-borne noise occurs when wall, floor, or other building elements are set into vibration by direct contact with vibrating sources such as mechanical equipment or domestic appliances. A small, vibrating pipe firmly attached to a plywood or gypsum wall panel will amplify the vibration noise. An illustration of this amplification of structure-borne noise is provided by the sound board of a piano. The major sources of structure-borne noise are the impact of walking on wood floors or of slamming doors, plumbing system noises, heating and air-conditioning system noises, noise from mechanical equipment or appliances, and vibration from sources outside the building. If the vibration is severe enough, it may have adverse effects not only on the occupants of a building but also on the building structure. Household appliances such as refrigerators, washing machines, sewing machines, clothes dryers, televisions, and pianos should be vibration isolated from the floor by means of rubber mounts placed under them if disturbing structure-borne noise is to be avoided. Residents should also be cautioned against locating these noise sources along party walls and in particular against mounting these appliances and kitchen cabinets directly on party walls so that the walls act as sounding boards in adjoining apartments. Window air-conditioners should be completely vibration isolated from the surrounding window frame by rubber gaskets and padding. The importance of isolating a vibrating source from the structure in the control of equipment noise cannot be overemphasized.

Another source of disturbing structure-borne noise is squeaking of wood floors. Some squeaks can be eliminated by lubricating the tongues of wood floor boards with mineral oil applied sparingly to the openings between adjacent boards. Loose finish flooring may be securely fastened to subflooring by surface nailing into the

Figure 11. Flanking Transmission of Impact and Structure-borne Noise

subfloor and preferably the joists. Ring-type nails or sawtooth staples properly spaced should be used in nailing finish flooring to subflooring. In an exposed joist structure, where finish flooring is warped, driving screws up through the subfloor and into the finish floor will be effective in drawing the layers of flooring tightly together to reduce noise.

Of course, noise caused by the impact of walking or scraping can be substantially reduced by the use of carpets. In the case of door slams, the impact noise may be eliminated by the use of door closers or rubber bumpers.

The noisy hammering of a plumbing system is usually caused by the sudden interruption of water-flow, for example, by a quick closing or opening of a tap.

Air chambers can be built into the plumbing system to reduce water hammer. The air pockets, rubber inserts, or spring elements in air chambers act to reduce noise. Air chambers are explained in Chapter 6.

Defective, loose, or worn valve stems create intense chattering of the plumbing system. The defective device can frequently be found without difficulty, since immediate use of the device causes the vibration, which generally occurs at some low-flow-velocity setting and diminishes or disappears at a higher flow setting. For example, if a chattering noise occurs when a particular faucet or tap is opened partially and diminishes when fully opened, the faucet more than likely has some loose or defective parts and should be repaired.

Noise can be a very complex problem. The housing inspector is not expected to be an acoustics expert. Nor is he expected to be able to analyze and solve the noise problems that an acoustics consultant would normally handle. He can, however, help teach the public that the annoyances and stress caused by noise can be partially alleviated by a simple awareness of common noise problems found in many residences.

Although the housing inspector is not an expert in the fields of zoning, plumbing, building, and electrical systems, he should be familiar with the applicable code in each of the respective fields. Familiarization with these codes will better enable him to recognize violations.

ELECTRICAL ASPECTS OF A HOUSING INSPECTION

TABLE OF CONTENTS

		Page
I.	Definitions	1
II.	Flow of Electric Current	2
III.	Electric Service Entrance	4
IV.	Grounding	6
V.	Two- or Three-Way Electric Services	7
VI.	Residential Wiring Adequacy	8
VII.	Wire Size and Types	8
VIII.	Electric Service Panel	10
IX.	Overcurrent Devices	11
X.	Electric Circuits	13
XI.	Common Electrical Violations	16
XII.	Steps Involved in Actual Inspections	18
XIII.	Wattage Consumption of Electrical Appliances	20
XIV.	Motor Currents	20

ELECTRICAL ASPECTS OF A HOUSING INSPECTION

There are two basic codes concerned with residential wiring that are of importance to the housing inspector. The first is the local electrical code. The purpose of this code is to safeguard persons and buildings and their contents from hazards arising from the use of electricity for light, heat, and power. The electrical code contains basic minimum provisions considered necessary for safety. Compliance with this code and proper maintenance will result in an installation essentially free from hazard but not necessarily efficient, convenient, or adequate for good service or future expansion.

The majority of local electrical codes are modeled after the National Electrical Code, published by the National Fire Prevention Association.

Just because an electrical installation was safe and adequate under the provisions of the electrical code at the time of installation does not indicate that the system is safe and adequate for use today. Hazards often occur because of overloading of wiring systems by methods or usage not in conformity with the code. This occurs because initial wiring did not provide for increases in the use of electricity. For this reason it is recommended that the initial installation be adequate and that reasonable provisions for system changes be made as may be required for future increase in the use of electricity.

The other code that contains electrical provisions is the local housing code. It establishes minimum standards for artificial and natural lighting and ventilation, specifies the minimum number of electric outlets and lighting fixtures per room, and prohibits temporary wiring except under certain circumstances. In addition, the housing code usually requires that all components of the electrical system be installed and maintained in a safe condition so as to prevent fire or electric shock.

This chapter contains electrical terms and major features of a residential wiring system that should be familiar to the housing inspector. It also contains a review of the steps involved in the electrical inspection, as well as commonly found conditions.

I. Definitions

A **Electricity** - is energy that can be used to run household appliances; it can produce light and heat, shocks, and numerous other effects.

B **Current** - the flow of electricity through a circuit.

  1 **Alternating current** is an electrical current that reverses its direction of flow at regular intervals: For example, it would alternate 60 times every second in a 60-cycle system. This type of power is commonly found in homes.

  2 **Direct current** is an electric current flowing in one direction. This type of current is not commonly found in today's homes.

C **Ampere** - the unit used in measuring intensity of flow of electricity. Symbol for it is "I."

D **Volt** - the unit for measuring electrical pressure or force, which is known as electromotive force. Symbol for it is "E."

E **Watt** - is the unit of electric power. Volts X Amperes = Watts.

F **Circuit** - the flow of electricity through two or more wires from the supply source to one or more outlets and back to the source.

G **Circuit Breaker** - a safety device used to break the flow of electricity by opening the circuit automatically in the event of overloading or used to open or close it manually.

H **Short Circuit** - is a break in the flow of electricity through a circuit due to the load caused by improper connection between hot and neutral wires (have the electrical inspector check for its location).

I **Conductor** - any substance capable of conveying an electric current. In the home, copper wire is usually used.

    1 **Bare conductor** is one with no insulation or covering.

    2 **Covered conductor** is one covered with one or more layers of insulation.

J **Fuse** - a safety device that cuts off the flow of electricity when the current flowing through the fuse exceeds its rated capacity.

K **Ground** - to connect with the earth as to ground an electric wire directly to the earth or indirectly through a water pipe or some other conductor. Usually a green-colored wire is used for grounding the whole electrical system to the earth. A white wire is then usually used to ground individual electrical components of the whole system.

L **Conductor Gauge** - a numerical system used to label electric conductor sizes, given in American Wire Gauge (AWG). The larger the AWG number the smaller the wire size.

M **Hot Wires** - those that carry the electric current or power to the load; they are usually black or red.

N **Service** - the conductor and equipment for delivering energy from the electricity supply system to the wiring system of the premises.

O **Service Drop** - the overhead service connectors from the last pole or other aerial support to and including the splices, if any, connecting to the service entrance conductors at the building or other structure.

P **Insulator** - a material that will not permit the passage of electricity.

Q **Neutral Wire** - the third wire in a three-wire distribution circuit; it is usually white or light gray and is connected to the ground.

R **Service Panel** - main panel or cabinet through which electricity is brought to building and distributed. It contains the main disconnect switch and fuses or circuit breakers.

S **Voltage Drop** - a voltage loss when wires carry current. The longer the cord the greater the voltage drop.

II. Flow of Electric Current

Electricity is usually generated by a generator that converts mechanical energy into electrical energy. The electricity is then run through a transformer where voltage is increased to several hundred thousand volts and in some instances to a million or more volts. This high voltage is necessary in order to increase the efficiency of power transmission over long distances.

This high-transmission voltage is then stepped down (reduced) to normal 115/230-volt household current by a transformer located near the point of use (residence). The electricity is then transmitted to the house by a series of wires called a "service drop." In areas where the electric wiring is underground, the wires leading to the building are buried in the ground.

In order for electric current to flow, it must travel from a higher to a lower potential voltage. In an electrical system the hot wires (black or red) are at a higher potential than the neutral or ground wire (white or green). Therefore, current will flow between the hot wires and the neutral or ground wires.

The voltage is a measure of the force at which electricity is delivered. It is similar to pressure in a water supply system.

Current is measured in amperes and is the quantity of flow of electricity. It is similar to measuring water in gallons per second.

A watt is equal to volts times amperes. It is a measure of how much power is flowing. Electricity is sold in quantities of watt-hours.

The earth, by virtue of moisture contained within the soil, serves as a very effective conductor. Therefore, in power transmission, instead of having both the hot and neutral wires carried by the transmission poles, one lead of the generator is connected to the ground, which serves as a conductor (see Figure 1). Only hot wires are carried by the transmission towers. At the house, or point where the electricity is to be used, the circuit is completed by another connection to ground.

The electric power utility provides a ground somewhere in its local distribution system; therefore, there is a ground wire in addition to the hot wires within the service drop. In Figure 1 this ground can be seen at the power pole that contains the stepdown transformer.

In addition to the ground connection provided by the electric utility, every building is required to have an independent ground, called a "system ground."

The system ground provides for limiting the voltage upon the circuit, which might otherwise occur through exposure to lighting, or for limiting the maximum potential to ground due to normal voltage. Therefore, the system ground's main purpose is to protect the electric system itself and offer limited protection to the user.
The system ground serves the same purpose as the power company's ground, however, being closer to the building, it has a lower resistance.

Figure 1. Electrical Power Flow

The "equipment ground," which we will discuss later in this chapter, protects man from potential harm during the use of certain electrical equipment.

The system ground should be a continuous wire of low resistance and of sufficient size to conduct current safely from lightning and overloads.

III. Electric Service Entrance

A Service Drop

The "Entrance Head" (see Figure 2) should be attached to the building at least 10 feet above ground, to prevent accidental contact by people. The conductor should clear all roofs by at least 8 feet and residential driveways by 12 feet. For public streets, alleys, roads, and driveways on other than residential property the clearance must be 18 feet.

The wires or conductor should be of sufficient size to carry the load and not smaller than No. 8 copper or equivalent.

Figure 2. Entrance Head

For connecting wire from the entrance head to the service drop wires, the National Electrical Code requires that the service entrance conductors be installed either (1) below the level of the service head, or (2) below the termination of the service-entrance cable sheath. Drip loops must be formed on individual conductors. This will prevent water from entering the electric service system.

The wires that form "entrance cable" should extend 36 inches from the entrance head, to provide a sufficient length to connect service drop wires to the building with insulators (see Figure 2).

The entrance cable may be a special type of armored outdoor type of wire or it may be enclosed in a conduit. The electric power meter may be located either within or outside the building. In either instance, the meter must be located before the main power disconnect.

Figure 3 shows an armored cable service entrance. The armored cable is anchored to the building with metal straps spaced every 4 feet. The cable is run down the wall and through a hole drilled through the building. The cable is then connected to the service panel, which should be located within 1 foot of where the cable enters the building.

The ground wire need not be insulated. This ground wire may be either solid or stranded copper, or a material with an equivalent resistance.

Figure 3. Service Entrance, Armored Cable

Figure 4 shows the use of thin-wall conduit in a service entrance.

Figure 4. Service Entrance Conduit Type

B Underground Service

When wires are run underground they must be protected from moisture and physical damage. The opening in the building foundation where the underground service enters the building must be moisture proof. Local codes should be referred to, concerning allowable materials for this type of service entrance.

C Electric Meter

The electric meter may be located inside or outside the building, as shown in Figure 3 or 4. The meter itself is weatherproof and is plugged into a weatherproof socket (see Figure 5). The electric power company furnishes the meter, the socket may or may not be furnished by the power company.

151

IV. Grounding

The system ground consists of grounding the neutral incoming wire as well as the neutral wire of the branch circuits. The equipment ground consists of grounding the metal parts of the service entrance, such as the service switch, as well as the service entrance conduit, armor, or cable.

The usual ground connection is to a water pipe of the city water system. The connection should be made to the street side of the cold water meter as shown in Figure 6.

If the water meter is located near the street curb, then the ground connection should be made to the cold water pipe as close as possible to where it enters the building.

Figure 5. Electric Meter

A typical weatherproof electric meter and its socket

Figure 6. View of a Typical Service Entrance

It is not unusual for a water meter to be removed from a building for service. If the ground connection is made at a point in the water piping system on the building side of the water meter, the ground circuit will be broken upon removal of the meter. This broken ground circuit represents a shock hazard if both sides of the water meter connections should be touched simultaneously.

In some instances the connections between the water meter to pipes are electrically very poor. In this case, if the ground connection is made on the building side of the water meter, there may not be an effective ground.

In order to prevent the two aforementioned situations the code requires that an effective bonding shall be provided around any equipment that is likely to be disconnected for repairs or replacement. This is illustrated in Figure 7. The same jumper arrangement would be required for a water meter that is installed near the curb. In many installations the water meter mounting bracket is designed to serve as an electric jumper.

Often an amateur mechanic, in the process of doing a household repair, will disconnect the house ground. Therefore, the housing inspector should always check the house ground to see if it is properly connected.

Figure 8 shows a typical grounding scheme at the service box of a residence. In this figure, only the grounded neutral wires are shown. The neutral strap is an uninsulated metal strip that is riveted directly to the service box. The ground wires from the service entrance, branch circuits, and house ground are joined by this strip.

When a city water supply is not available for grounding, a substitute must be made. The most common ground is a pipe or rod that is driven into the ground a distance of at least 8 feet. If the pipe is made of steel or iron, it must be 3/4 inch in diameter and galvanized. A copper ground pipe of 1/2 inch diameter is sufficient.

The code requires that a ground rod be entirely independent of and kept at least 6 feet from any other ground of the type used for radio, telephone, or lightning rods.

V. Two- or Three-Wire Electric Services

One of the wires in every installation is grounded. This neutral wire is always white. The hot wires are usually black or red or some other color, but never white.

The potential difference or voltage between the hot wires and the ground or neutral of a normal residential electrical system is 115

Figure 7. Water Meter Jumper

A Jumper Must be instlled Around a Water Meter if the House Ground Connection is Made on the House Side of the Water Meter

Figure 8. Typical Grounding Scheme at Entrance

Typical grounding scheme at entrance switch of residental installation. only the grounded neutral wires are shown The detail used varies in different localities

Figure 9. Ground Connection

volts. Thus, where we have a two-wire installation (one hot and one neutral) only 115-volt power is available (see Figure 9).

When three wires are installed (two hot and one neutral) either 115- or 230-volt power is available. In a three-wire system the voltage between the neutral and either of the hot wires is 115; between the two hot wires it is 230 volts.

The major advantage of a three-wire system is that it permits the operation of heavy electrical equipment such as laundry dryers, cooking ranges, and air conditioners, the majority of which require 230-volt circuits. In addition, the three-wire system is split at the service panel into two 115-volt systems to supply power for small appliances and electric lights. The result is a doubling of the number of circuits, and possibly a corresponding increase in the number of branch circuits, with a reduction of the probability of fire caused by overloading electrical circuits.

VI. Residential Wiring Adequacy

The use of electricity in the home has risen sharply since the 1930's. Many home owners have failed to repair or improve their wiring to keep it safe and up to date. The National Electrical Code recommends that individual residences be provided with a minimum of 100-ampere three-wire service. This type service is sufficient in a one-family house or dwelling unit to provide safe and adequate electric supply for the lighting, refrigerator, iron, and an 8,000-watt cooking range, plus other appliances requiring a total of up to 10,000 watts altogether.

Some homes have a 60-ampere, three-wire service. It is recommended that these homes be rewired for at least the minimum of 100 amperes recommended in the National Code since they are safely capable of supplying current only for lighting and portable appliances such as a cooking range and regular dryer (4,500 watts), or an electric hot-water heater (2,500 watts) and cannot handle additional major appliances.

Other homes today have only a 30-ampere, 115-volt, two-wire service. This system can safely handle only a limited amount of lighting, a few minor appliances, and no major appliances. Therefore, this size service is substandard in terms of modern household needs for electricity. Furthermore, it constitutes a fire hazard and a threat to the safety of the home and the occupants.

VII. Wire Size and Types

A Wire Size

Electric power flows over wire. It flows with relative ease (little resistance) in some materials such as copper and with a substantial amount of resistance in iron. If iron wire were used it would have to be 10 times as large as copper wire.

Copper wire sizes are indicated by a number. No. 14 is most commonly used in residential branch circuits. No. 14 is the smallest permitted by the Code for use in a branch circuit with a 15-ampere capacity. No. 16, 18, and 20 are progressively smaller than No. 14 and are usually used for extension wires. As the number of the wire becomes smaller the size and current capacity of the wire increases. No. 1 is the heaviest wire usually used in ordinary household wiring.

Wire of correct size must be used for two reasons: current capacity and voltage drop.

1. When current flows through a wire it creates heat. The greater the amount of flow, the greater the amount of heat generated. (Doubling the amperes without changing the wire size increases the amount of heat by four times.) The heat is electric energy that has been converted into heat energy by the resistance of the wire; the heat created by the coils in a toaster is an example. This heat developed in an electrical conductor is wasted, and thus the electric energy used to generate it is wasted. If the amount of heat generated by the flow of current through the wire becomes excessive, a fire may result. Therefore, the code sets the maximum permissible current that may flow through a certain type and size wire.
   The following are examples of current capacities for copper wire of various sizes.

Size wire (AWG)	#14	#12	#10	#8
Max. capacity, amperes	15	20	30	40

2. In addition to heat generation there will be a reduction in voltage as a result of attempting to force more current through a wire than it is capable of carrying. Certain appliances, such as induction-type electric motors, may be damaged if operated at too low a voltage.

B   Wire Types

1. **Wire markings** - All wires must be marked to indicate the maximum working voltage, the proper type letter or letters for the type wire specified in the code, the manufacturer's name or trademark, and the AWG size or circular-mil area.
2. **Insulations used** There are a variety of wire types which can be used for a wide range of temperature and moisture conditions. The 1975 National Electrical Code should be consulted to determine the proper wire for specific conditions.

C   Types of Cable

1. **Nonmetallic Sheathed Cable** - This type of cable consists of wires wrapped in a paper layer, followed by another spiral layer of paper, and enclosed in a fabric braid, which is treated with moisture-resistant and fire-resistant compounds. Figure 10 shows this type of cable, which often is marketed under the "Romex" name. This type of cable can be used only indoors and in permanently dry locations.

2. **Armored Cable** - This type of cable is commonly known by the BX or Flex-steel trade names. Wires are wrapped in a tough paper and covered with a strong spiral flexible steel armor. This type of cable is shown in Figure 11 and may be used only in permanently dry indoor locations. Armored cable must be supported by a strap or staple every 6 feet and within 24 inches of every switch or junction box, except for concealed runs in old work where it is impossible to mount straps.

3. **Other Cable** Cables are also available with other outer coatings of metals such as copper, bronze, and aluminum for use in a variety of conditions.

D   Flexible Cords

Flexible cords are used to connect lamps, appliances, and other devices to outlets. Each wire consists of many strands of fine wire for flexibility. Extension cords in AWG sizes 16 to 18 are usually fine for lamps and smaller appliances, if the cord is not too long. A commonly accepted standard limits their length to 8 feet of unspliced cord. This keeps the cords short enough to prevent the excessive voltage drops, minimizes the possibility of fire caused by overheating of the wire due to overload, and also minimizes the danger of someone's tripping over them.

E   Open Wiring

Open wiring is a wiring method using knobs, nonmetallic tubes, cleats, and flexible tubing for the protection and support of insulated conductors in or on buildings and not concealed by the structure. The term "open wiring" does not mean exposed, bare wiring. In dry locations when not exposed to severe

Figure 10. Nonmetallic Sheath Cable

Figure 11. Armored Cable

physical damage, conductors may be separately encased in flexible tubing. Tubing should be in continuous lengths not exceeding 15 feet and secured to the surface by straps not more than 4 1/2 feet apart. They should be separated from other conductors by at least 2 1/2 inches and should have a permanently maintained airspace between them and any and all pipes they cross.

F   Concealed Knob and Tube Wiring

Concealed knob and tube wiring is a wiring method using knobs, tubes, and flexible nonmetallic tubing for the protection and support of insulated wires concealed in hollow spaces of walls and ceilings of buildings. This wiring method is similar to open wiring, and like open wiring, is usually found only in older buildings.

VIII. Electric Service Panel

Service Switch
This is a main switch that will disconnect the entire electrical system at one

time. The main fuses or circuit breakers are usually located within the "Service Switch" box. The branch circuit fuse or circuit breaker may also be located within this box.

According to the code, the switch must be "externally operable." This condition is fulfilled if the switch can be operated without the operator's being exposed to electrically active parts. Older switches use external handles as shown in Figure 12.

Most of today's service switches do not have hinged switch blades. Instead, the main fuse is mounted on a small insulated block that can be pulled out of the switch. When this block is removed, the circuit is broken just as if the blades had been operated with a handle.

The neutral terminal or wire of a grounded circuit must never be interrupted by a fuse or circuit breaker. In some installations the service switch is a "solid neutral" switch. This means that the neutral wire in the switch is not broken by the switch or a fuse.

When circuit breakers instead of fuses are used in homes, the use of main circuit breakers may or may not be required. If it takes not more than six movements of the hand to open all the branch-circuit breakers, no main breaker or switch or fuse will be required ahead of the branch-circuit breakers. Thus, a house with seven or more branch circuits requires a separate disconnect means or a main circuit breaker ahead of the branch-circuit breakers (see Figure 13).

IX. Overcurrent Devices

The amperage (current flow) in any wire is limited to the maximum permitted by using an overcurrent device of a

Figure 12. Two Wire Single Phase Grounded Service Panel (Fuse Type)

specific size as specified by the code. Two types of overcurrent devices are in common use: circuit breakers and fuses; both are rated in amperes. The overcurrent device must be rated at equal or lower capacity than the wire of the circuit it protects.

A Circuit Breakers (Fuseless) Service Panels

A circuit breaker (see Figure 14) looks something like an ordinary electric light switch. There is a handle that may be used to turn power on or off. Inside is a simple mechanism that, in case of a circuit overload, trips the switch and breaks the circuit. The circuit breaker may be reset by simply flipping the switch. A circuit breaker is capable of taking harmless short-period overloads (such as the heavy initial current required in the starting of a washing machine or air conditioner) without tripping but protects against prolonged overloads. After the cause of trouble

Figure 13. Three Wire Grounded Single Phase Circuit Beaker Service Panel

has been located and corrected, the power is easily restored by flipping the circuit breaker switch (circuit breakers are modern substitutes for fuses). Fuseless service panels are usually broken up into the following circuits.

1. A 100-ampere or larger main circuit breaker that shuts off all power.
2. A 40-ampere circuit for an appliance such as an electric cooking range. against the dangers of overloading
3. A 30-ampere circuit for clothes dryer, hot water heater, or central air conditioning.
4. A 20-ampere circuit for kitchen, small appliances, and power tools.
5. A 15-ampere circuit for general purpose lighting, TV, and vacuum cleaner.
6. Space for circuits to be added if needed for future use.

B Fused Ampere Service Panel or Fuse Box

Fuse-type panel boxes are generally found in older homes. They are equally as safe and adequate as a circuit breaker of equivalent capacity, provided fuses of the proper size are used.
A fuse (see Figure 15), like a circuit breaker, is designed to protect a circuit and short circuits and does this in two manners.

a. When a fuse is blown by a short circuit the metal strip is instantly heated to an extremely high temperature, and this heat causes it to vaporize. A fuse blown by a short circuit may be easily recognized because the window of the fuse usually becomes discolored.

b. In a fuse blown by overload the metal strip is melted at its weakest point, and this breaks the flow of current to the load. In this case the window of the fuse remains clear; therefore, a blown fuse caused by an overload may also be easily recognized.

Sometimes, although a fuse has not been blown, the bottom of the fuse may be severely discolored and pitted. This indicates a loose connection due to the fuse's not being screwed in properly.

Generally, all fused panel boxes are wired similarly for two- and three-wire systems. In a two-wire-circuit panel box the black or red hot wire is connected to a terminal of the main disconnect, and the white or light gray neutral wire is connected to the neutral strip, which is then grounded to the pipe on the street side of the water meter.
In a three-wire system the black and red hot wires are connected to separate terminals of the main disconnect, and the neutral wire is grounded the same as for a two-wire system

(see Figure 12). Below each fuse is a terminal to which a black or red wire is connected. The white or light gray neutral wires are then connected to the neutral strip. Each fuse indicates a separate circuit.

1. **Non-tamperable Fuses** - All ordinary plug fuses, shown in Figure 15, have the same diameter and physical appearance regardless of their current capacity. Thus, if a circuit designed for a 15-ampere fuse is overloaded so that the 15-ampere fuse blows out, nothing will prevent a person from replacing the 15-ampere fuse with a 20- or 30-ampere fuse, which may not blow out. If a circuit wired with No. 14 wire (current capacity 15 amperes) is fused with a 20- or 30-ampere fuse and an overload develops, more current than the No. 14 wire is safely capable of carrying could pass through the circuit. The result would be a heating of the wire and a potential fire.

Type S fuses, shown in Figure 15, have different lengths and diameter threads for each different amperage capacity. An adapter is first inserted into the ordinary fuse holder, which adapts the fuse holder for only one capacity fuse. Once the adapter is inserted, it cannot be removed.

2. **Cartridge Fuses**

Figure 15 shows two different types of cartridge fuses. A cartridge fuse protects an electric circuit in the same manner as an ordinary plug fuse already described protects it. Cartridge fuses are often used as main fuses.

X. Electric Circuits

An electric circuit in good repair carries electricity through two or three wires from the source of supply to an outlet and back to the source.

A **Branch Circuit**

A branch circuit is an electric circuit that supplies electric current to a limited number of electric outlets and fixtures. A residence generally has many branch circuits. Each is protected against short circuits and overloads by a 15- or 20-ampere fuse or circuit breaker.

The number of outlets per branch circuit varies from building to building. The code requires enough light circuits so that 3 watts of power will be available for each square foot of floor area

Figure 14. Circuit Breaker

Figure 15. Types of Fuses

Plug fuses are not made in ratings over 30 amp.

A typical Type-S non-tamperable fuse, and its adapter. Once an adapter has been screwed into a fuse-holder, it cannot be removed. This prevents use of fuses larger than originally intended.

Cartridge fuses rated 60 amps, or less are of the ferrule type shown.

Cartridge fuses rated more than 60 amp. have knife-blade terminals shown.

in a house. A circuit wired with No. 14 wire and protected by a 15-ampere overcurrent protection device provides 15 X 115 or 1,725 watts; each circuit is obviously enough for 1,725/3 or 575 square feet.

Note that 575 is a minimum figure; if future use is considered, 500 or even 400 square feet per branch circuit should be used.

B Special Appliance Circuits

The branch circuit will provide electric power for lighting, radio, television, and small portable appliances. However, the larger electric appliances usually found in the kitchen consume more power and must have their own special circuit.

Section 220-3b of the code requires two special circuits to serve only appliance outlets in kitchen, laundry, pantry, family-room, dining room, and breakfast room. Both circuits must be extended to the kitchen; the other rooms may be served by either one or both of these circuits. No lighting outlets may be connected to these circuits, and they must be wired with No. 12 wire and protected by a 20-ampere overcurrent device. Each circuit will have a capacity of 20 X 115 or 2,300 watts, which is not too much when one considers that toasters often require over 1,600 watts.

C Individual Appliance Circuits

It is customary to provide a circuit for each of the following appliances:

1. Range
2. Water heater
3. Automatic laundry
4. Clothes dryer

5   Garbage disposer
6   Dishwasher
7   Furnace
8   Water pump

Note that these circuits may be either 115 volts or 230 volts, depending on the particular appliance or motor installed.

D Outlet Switch and Junction Boxes

The code requires that every switch, outlet, and joint in wire or cable be housed in a box. Every fixture must be mounted on a box. Most boxes are made of metal with a galvanized finish. Figure 16 shows a typical outlet box.

When a cable of any style is used for wiring, the code requires that it be securely anchored with a connector to each box it enters.

E Grounding Outlets

An electrical appliance may appear to be in good repair, and yet it might be a danger to the user. Consider a portable electric drill. It consists of an electric motor inside a metal casing. When the switch is depressed, the current flows to the motor, and the drill rotates. As a result of wear, however, the insulation on the wire inside the drill may deteriorate and allow the hot side of the power cord to come in contact with the metal casing. This will not affect the operation of the drill.

A person fully clothed using the drill in the living room, which has a dry floor, will not receive a shock, even though he is in contact with the electrified drill case. His body is not grounded, because of the dry floor. If, however, the operator should be standing on a wet basement floor, his body might be grounded, and when he touches the electrified drill case, current will pass through his body.

In order to protect man, the drill case is usually connected to the system ground by means of a wire called an "appliance ground." In this instance, as the drill is plugged in, current will flow between the shorted hot wire and the drill case and cause the overcurrent device to break the circuit. Thus the appliance ground has protected man. The appliance ground is the third wire found on many appliances.

The appliance ground on the appliance will be of no use unless the outlet into which the appliance is plugged is grounded. The outlet is grounded by being in physical contact with a ground outlet box. The outlet box is grounded by having a third ground wire, or a grounded conduit, as part of the circuit wiring.

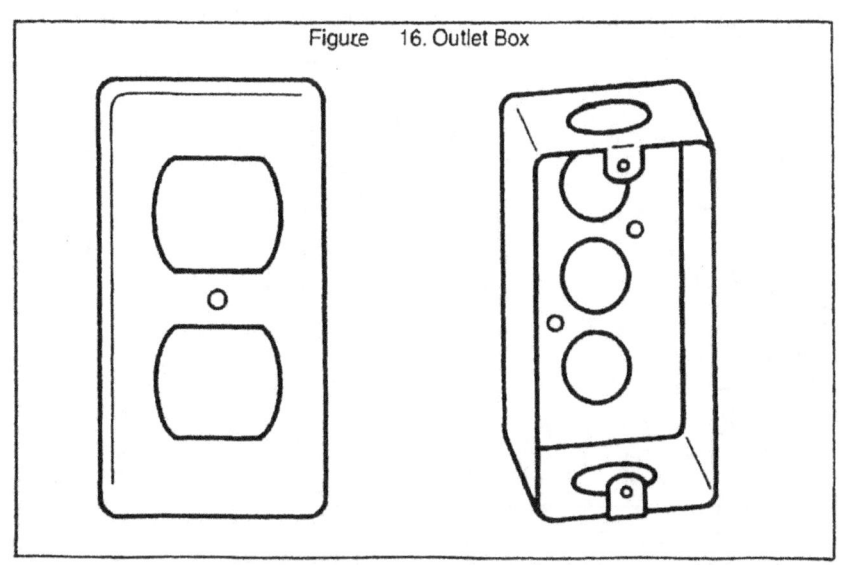

Figure 16. Outlet Box

All new buildings are required to have grounded outlets (as shown in Figure 17). The outlet may be tested by using a circuit tester. The circuit tester should light when both of its leads are plugged into the two elongated parallel openings of the outlet. In addition, the tester should light when one lead is plugged into the round third opening and the other is plugged into the hot side of the outlet.

If the conventional two-opening outlet is used, it still may be grounded. In this instance the screw that holds the outlet cover plate is the third-wire ground. The tester should light when one lead is in contact with a clean paint-free metal outlet cover plate screw and the hot side of the outlet. If the tester fails to light then the outlet is not grounded. If the outlet is not grounded then the tester will not function.

If a two-opening outlet is grounded, it may be adapted for use by a three-wire appliance by using an adapter. The loose-wire portion of the adapter should be secured behind the metal screw of the outlet plate cover.

Many appliances such as electric shavers and some new hand tools are double insulated and are safe without having a third ground wire.

XI. Common Electrical Violations

A The most apparent requirements that a housing inspector must check are the existence of the power supply; the types, locations, and conditions of the wiring in use; and the existence of the number of wall outlets or ceiling fixtures required by his local code and their condition. In making his investigations, these considerations will serve as useful guides:

1 **Power Supply** - Where is it located, is it grounded properly, and is it at least of minimum capacity required to supply current safely for lighting and the major and minor appliances in the dwelling?

Figure 17. Grounded Type Receptacle

The grounding type receptacle can be used with either 2-prong or 3-prong plugs.

This is "U" shaped section.

2. **Panel Box Covers or Doors** - These should be accessible only from the front and should be sealed in such a way that they can be operated safely without the danger of contact with live or exposed parts of the wiring system.

3. **Switch, Outlets, and Junction Boxes** - These also must be covered to protect against danger of electric shock.

4. **Frayed or Bare Wires** - These are usually the result of long use and a drying out and cracking of the insulation, which leave the wires exposed, or else a result of constant friction and rough handling of the wire, which cause it to fray or become bare. Wiring in this condition constitutes a safety hazard, and correction of such defects should be ordered immediately.

5. **Electric Cords Under Rugs or Other Floor Coverings** - Putting electric cords in locations such as these is prohibited because of the potential fire hazard caused by continuing contact over a period of time between these heat-bearing cords and the flammable floor coverings. Direct the occupant to shift the cords to a safe location, explain why, and make sure it is done before you leave.

6. **Bathroom Lighting** - It should include at least one permanently installed ceiling or wall light fixture with a wall switch and plate so located and maintained that there is no danger of short circuiting from use of other bathroom facilities or splashing of water. Fixture or cover plates should be insulated or grounded.

7. **Lighting of Public Hallways, Stairways, Landings, and Foyers** A common standard here is sufficient lighting to provide illumination of 10 foot-candles on every part of these areas at all times. Sufficient lighting means that a person can clearly see his feet on all parts of the stairways and halls. Every public hall and stairway in a structure containing *less* *than three* dwelling units may be supplied with conveniently located light switches controlling an adequate lighting system that may be turned on when needed, instead of full-time lighting.

8. **Habitable Room Lighting** - The standard here may be two floor convenience outlets although floor outlets are dangerous unless protected by proper dust and water covers or one convenience outlet and one wall or ceiling electric light fixture. This number constitutes an absolute and often inadequate minimum given the contemporary widespread use of electricity in the home. The minimum should be that number required to provide adequate lighting and power to accommodate lighting and appliances normally used in each room.

9. **Octopus Outlets or Wiring** - This term is applied to outlets into which plugs have been inserted and are being used to permit more than two lights or portable appliances, such as a TV, lamp, or radio, to be connected to the electrical system. The condition occurs where the number of outlets is insufficient to accommodate the normal use of the room. This practice overloads the circuit and is a potential source of fire, which may be caused by overloading the circuit.

10. **Outlet Covers** - Every outlet and receptacle must be covered by a protective plate to prevent contact of its wiring or terminals with the body, combustible object or splashing water.

The following items are conditions that cause needless dangers and must also be corrected:

a. **Excessive or faulty fusing** - The wire's capacity must not be exceeded by the fuse or circuit breaker capacity or be left unprotected by faulty fusing or circuit breakers. Fuses and circuit breakers are safety devices designed to "blow" as a means of protection against overloadings of the electrical system or one or more of its circuits. Pennies under fuses are put there to bypass the fuse. These are illegal and must be removed. Overfusing is done for the same reason. The latter can be prevented by the installation of modern fuse stats, which prevent use of any fuse of a higher amperage than can be handled by the circuit it serves.

b **Cords run through walls or doorways and hanging cords or wires** - This is a makeshift-type installation and most often is installed by an unqualified handyman or do-it-yourself occupant. The inspector should check with his local electrical section to determine the policy regarding this type of insulation and govern his action in accordance with the electrical section's policies.

c **Temporary wiring** - This type of installation should not be allowed, with the exception of extension cords that go directly from portable lights and electric fixtures to convenience outlets.

d **Excessively long extension cords** - This requirement does not apply to specially designed extension cords for operating portable tools and trouble lights. Cities operating under modern code standards limit the length of loose cords or extension lines to a maximum of 8 feet. This is necessary because those that are too long will overheat if overloaded or if a short circuit develops and thus create a fire hazard. Even shorter lengths are feasible in housing with new or updated wiring systems that include one convenience outlet every 12 feet around the perimeter of the room.

e **Dead or dummy outlets** - These are sometimes installed to deceive the inspection agency. This is why all outlets must be tested or the occupants questioned to see if these are alive and functioning properly. A dead outlet cannot be counted to determine compliance with the code.

XII. Steps Involved in Actual Inspection

A **Testing Tools**
The basic tools required by an inspector of housing for making an electrical inspection are a fuse and circuit tester and a flashlight.

B **Danger of Techniques**

The first thing is to remember you are in a strange house and the layout is unfamiliar to you. The second thing to remember is that you are dealing with electricity *take no chances.* Go to the water meter and check the ground. It should connect to the water line on the street side of the water meter or else be equipped with a jumper wire. Do not touch any box or wire until you are sure of the ground. Go to the main fuse box and check all fuses in all boxes. Note the condition of the wiring and of the box itself and check whether it is overfused or not. Examine all wiring in the cellar. Make sure you are standing in a dry spot before touching any electrical device. Do not disassemble the fuse box or other devices. Decisions must be made on what you see. If in doubt, consult your supervisor.

Make note whether any fuse boxes or junction boxes are uncovered. Examine all wiring for frayed or bare spots, improper splicing, or rotted, worn, or inadequate insulation. Avoid all careless touching. When in doubt DON'T! If you see bare wire, have the owner call an electrician. Look for wires or cords in use in the cellar. Many work benches are lighted by an old lamp that was once in the parlor and now has a spliced or badly frayed cord or both. Be certain all switch boxes and outlets are in a tight, sound condition.

Make sure that the emergency switch for the oil burner is at the top of the cellar stairs, not on top of the unit.

If you find an electric clothes washer-clothes dryer combination in a dwelling, it should have a 240-volt circuit 30-ampere service connected to a separate fuse or circuit breaker. Washer-dryer combinations and other portable appliances in the entire house should be served by sufficiently heavy service. If either of these special lines is not available under the above-stated conditions, consult your supervisor.

An electric range needs a 50-ampere circuit, 240 volts. A dishwasher needs a 20-ampere, 120-volt circuit. A separate three-wire circuit must be installed for an electric water heater. Continue your inspection this way through the house. In the bathroom look for the usual items, but also check for dangerous items such as radios or plug-in portable electric heaters. Have them removed immediately. Such items have killed thousands of people either has a spliced or badly frayed cord or both. Be certain all switch boxes and outlets are in a tight, sound condition. Make sure that the emergency switch for the oil burner is at the top of the cellar stairs, not on top of the unit.

If you find an electric clothes washer-clothes dryer combination in a dwelling, it should have a 240-volt circuit 30-ampere service connected to a separate fuse or circuit breaker. Washer-dryer combinations and other portable appliances in the entire house should be served by sufficiently heavy service. If either of these special lines is not available under the above-stated conditions, consult your supervisor.

An electric range needs a 50-ampere circuit, 240 volts. A dishwasher needs a 20-ampere, 120-volt circuit. A separate three-wire circuit must be installed for an electric water heater. Continue your inspection this way through the because they touched them after getting out of the bathtub or shower while still wet or because the appliance fell into the water. Look for brass pull chains in bathroom lighting fixtures. If one exists, have owner attach a string to the end of it as a temporary precaution, then order it replaced with a wall switch as required by the electrical code.

To sum up, in broad terms, the housing inspector's investigation of specified electrical elements in a house is made to detect any obvious evidence of an insufficient power supply, to ensure the availability of adequate and safe lighting and electrical facilities, and to discover and correct any obvious hazard. Because electricity is a technical, complicated field, the housing inspector, when in doubt, should consult his supervisor. He cannot, however, close the case until appropriate corrective action has been taken on all such referrals.

XIII. Wattage Consumption of Electrical Appliances

(100 watts = approximately 1 ampere)

Appliance	Watts
Air conditioner (central)	5,000
Air conditioner (window)	see name plate
Blanket	150
Blender	250
Chaffing Dish	600
Clock	3
Coffee Maker	600
Deep fryer	1,320
Dishwasher	1,800
Egg boiler	250
Electric shaver	10
Fan	75
Food mixer	200
Furnace (fuel fixed)	800
Frying pan	600
Garbage disposer	900
Griddle	1,300
Grill	600
Heater (radiant)	1,600
Heating pad	50
Hot-plate (2 burners)	1,650
Humidifier	500
Immersion heater	300
Iron	1,000
Ironer	1,650
Lighting	
Bed lamp	40
Ceiling light	100
Decorative lights	80
Dining light	150
Dresser lamps	60
Drop light	60
Floor lamp	400
Fluorescent	80
Sun lamp	275
Table lamp	100

Appliance	Watts
Radio	100
Range	8,000 to 16,000
Refrigerator	250
Roaster (large)	1,380
Rotisserie	1,400
Sewing machine	75
Soldering iron	200
Stereo hi-fi	300
Sump pump	300
Television	300
Toaster	1,100
Vacuum cleaner	400
Waffle iron	660
Washing machine	5,200
Water heater	2,500-4,500
Water pump	300

XIV. Motor Currents

Horsepower	Full load amperes			
	115 v	230 1-phase	230 2-phase	230 3-phase
1/4	5.8	2.9		
1/2	9.8	4.9	2.0	2.0
3/4	13.8	6.9	2.4	2.8
1	16.0	8.0	3.2	3.6

PLUMBING ELEMENTS OF A HOUSING INSPECTION

CONTENTS

	PAGE
I. Background Factors	1
II. Definitions	1
III. Main Features of an Indoor Plumbing System	3
IV. Elements of a Plumbing System	3

PLUMBING ELEMENTS OF A HOUSING INSPECTION

Plumbing may be defined as practice, materials, and fixtures used in the installation, maintenance, and alteration of all piping, fixtures, appliances, and appurtenances in connection with sanitary or storm drainage facilities, the venting system, and the public or private water supply systems. **Plumbing** does not include the trade of drilling water wells, installing water softening equipment, or the business of manufacturing or selling plumbing fixtures, appliances, equipment, or hardware. A plumbing system consists of three separate parts: an adequate potable water supply system; a safe, adequate drainage system; and ample fixtures and equipment.

I. Background Factors

The generalized inspector of housing is concerned with a safe water supply system, an adequate drainage system, and ample and proper fixtures and equipment. This chapter covers the major features of a residential plumbing system and the basic plumbing terms the inspector must know and understand to identify properly housing code violations involving plumbing and the more complicated defects that he will refer to the appropriate agencies.

II. Definitions

1. **Air Chambers** — Air Chambers are pressure absorbing devices that eliminate water hammer. They should be installed as close as possible to the valves or faucet and at the end of long runs of pipe.

2. **Air Gap (Drainage System)** — The unobstructed vertical distance through the free atmosphere between the outlet of a water pipe and the flood level rim of the receptacle into which it is discharging.

3. **Air Gap (Water Distribution System)** — The unobstructed vertical distance through the free atmosphere between the lowest opening from any pipe or faucet supplying water to a tank, plumbing fixture, or other device and the flood level rim of the receptacle.

4. **Air Lock** — An air lock is a bubble of air which restricts the flow of water in a pipe.

5. **Backflow** — Backflow is the flow of water or other liquids, mixtures, or substances into the distributing pipes of a potable water supply from any source or sources other than the intended source. Back siphonage is one type of backflow.

6. **Back Siphonage** — Back siphonage is the flowing back of used, contaminated, or polluted water from a plumbing fixture or vessel into a potable water supply due to a negative pressure in the pipe.

7. **Branch** — A branch is any part of the piping system other than the main, riser, or stack.

8. **Branch Vent** — A vent connecting one or more individual vents with a vent stack.

9. **Building Drain** — The building (house) drain is the part of the lowest piping of a drainage system that receives the discharge from soil, waste, or other drainage pipes inside the walls of the building (house) and conveys it to the building sewer beginning 3 feet outside the building wall.

10. **Cross Connection** — Any physical connection or arrangement between two otherwise separate piping systems, one of which contains potable water and the other either water of unknown or questionable safety or steam, gas, or chemical whereby there may be a flow from one system to the other, the direction of flow depending on the pressure differential between the two systems. (See Backflow and Back siphonage.)

11. **Disposal Field** — An area containing a series of one or more trenches lined with coarse aggregate and conveying the effluent from the septic tank through vitrified clay pipe or

perforated, non-metallic pipe, laid in such a manner that the flow will be distributed with reasonable uniformity into natural soil.

12 **Drain** — A drain is any pipe that carries waste water or water-borne waste in a building (house) drainage system.

13 **Flood Level Rim** — The top edge of a receptacle from which water overflows.

14 **Flushometer Valve** — A device that discharges a predetermined quantity of water to fixtures for flushing purposes and is closed by direct water pressures.

15 **Flush Valve** — A device located at the bottom of the tank for flushing water closets and similar fixtures.

16 **Grease Trap** — See Interceptor

17 **Hot Water** — Hot water means potable water that is heated to at least 120°F and used for cooking, cleaning, washing dishes, and bathing.

18 **Insanitary** — Contrary to sanitary principles — injurious to health.

19 **Interceptor** — A device designed and installed so as to separate and retain deleterious, hazardous, or undesirable matter from normal wastes and permit normal sewage or liquid wastes to discharge into the drainage system by gravity.

20 **Leader** — An exterior drainage pipe for conveying storm water from roof or gutter drains to the building storm drain, combined building sewer, or other means of disposal.

21 **Main Vent** — The principal artery of the venting system, to which vent branches may be connected.

22 **Main Sewer** — See Public Sewer.

23 **Pneumatic** — The word pertains to devices making use of compressed air as in pressure tanks boosted by pumps.

24 **Potable Water** — Water having no impurities present in amounts sufficient to cause disease or harmful physiological effects and conforming in its bacteriological and chemical quality to the requirements of the Public Health Service drinking water standards or meeting the regulations of the public health authority having jurisdiction.

25 **P & T (Pressure and Temperature) Relief Valve** — A safety valve installed on a hot water storage tank to limit temperature and pressure of the water.

26 **P Trap** — A trap with a vertical inlet and a horizontal outlet.

27 **Public Sewer** — A common sewer directly controlled by public authority.

28 **Relief Vent** — An auxiliary vent that permits additional circulation of air in or between drainage and vent systems.

29 **Septic Tank** — A watertight receptacle that receives the discharge of a building's sanitary drain system or part thereof and is designed and constructed so as to separate solid from the liquid, digest organic matter through a period of detention, and allow the liquids to discharge into the soil outside of the tank through a system of open-joint or perforated piping, or through a seepage pit.

30 **Sewerage System** — A sewerage system comprises all piping, appurtenances, and treatment facilities used for the collection and disposal of sewage, except plumbing inside and in connection with buildings served, and the building drain.

31 **Soil Pipe** — The pipe that directs the sewage of a house to the receiving sewer, building drain, or building sewer.

32 **Soil Stack** — The vertical piping that terminates in a roof vent and carries off the vapors of a plumbing system.

33 **Stack Vent** — An extension of a solid or waste stack above the highest horizontal drain connected to the stack. Sometimes called a waste vent or a soil vent.

34 **Storm Sewer** — A sewer used for conveying rain water, surface water, condensate, cooling water, or similar liquid waste.

35 Trap — A trap is a fitting or device that provides a liquid seal to prevent the emission of sewer gases without materially affecting the flow of sewage or waste water through it.

36 Vacuum Breaker — A device to prevent backflow (back siphonage) by means of an opening through which air may be drawn to relieve negative pressure (vacuum).

37 Vent Stack — The vertical vent pipe installed to provide air circulation to and from the drainage system and that extends through one or more stories.

38 Water Hammer — The loud thump of water in a pipe when a valve or faucet is suddenly closed.

39 Water Service Pipe — The pipe from the water main or other sources of potable water supply to the water-distributing system of the building served.

40 Water Supply System — The water supply system consists of the water service pipe, the water-distributing pipes, the necessary connecting pipes, fittings, control valves, and all appurtenances in or adjacent to the building or premises.

41 Wet Vent — A vent that receives the discharge of waste other than from water closets.

42 Yoke Vent — A pipe connecting upward from a soil or waste stack to a vent stack for the purpose of preventing pressure changes in the stacks.

III. Main Features of an Indoor Plumbing System

The primary functions of the plumbing system within the house are as follows:

1 To bring an adequate and potable supply of hot and cold water to the users of the dwelling.

2 To drain all waste water and sewage discharged from these fixtures into the public sewer, or private disposal system.

It is, therefore, very important that the housing inspector familiarize himself fully with all elements of these systems so that he may recognize inadequacies of the structure's plumbing as well as other code violations. In order to aid the inspector in understanding the plumbing system, a series of drawings and diagrams has been included at the end of this chapter.

IV. Elements of a Plumbing System

A Supply System

1 Water Service: The piping of a house service line should be as short as possible. Elbows and bends should be kept to a minimum since these reduce the pressure and therefore the supply of water to fixtures in the house.

The house service line should also be protected from freezing. The burying of the line under 4 feet of soil is a commonly accepted depth to prevent freezing. This depth varies, however, across the country from north to south. The local or state plumbing code should be consulted for the recommended depth in your area of the country.

A typical house service installation is pictured in Figure 1.

The materials used for a house service may be copper, cast iron, steel or wrought iron. The connections used should be compatible with the type of pipe used.

a Corporation stop — The corporation stop is connected to the water main. This connection is usually made of brass and can be connected to the main by use of a special tool without shutting off the municipal supply. The valve incorporated in the corporation stop permits the pressure to be maintained in the main while the service to the building is completed.

b Curb stop — The curb stop is a similar valve used to isolate the building from the main for repairs, nonpayment of water bills, or flooded basements.

Since the corporation stop is usually under the street and would necessitate breaking the pavement to reach the valve, the curb stop is used as the isolation valve.

c Curb stop box — The curb stop box is an access box to the curb stop for opening and closing the valve. A long-handled wrench is used to reach the valve.

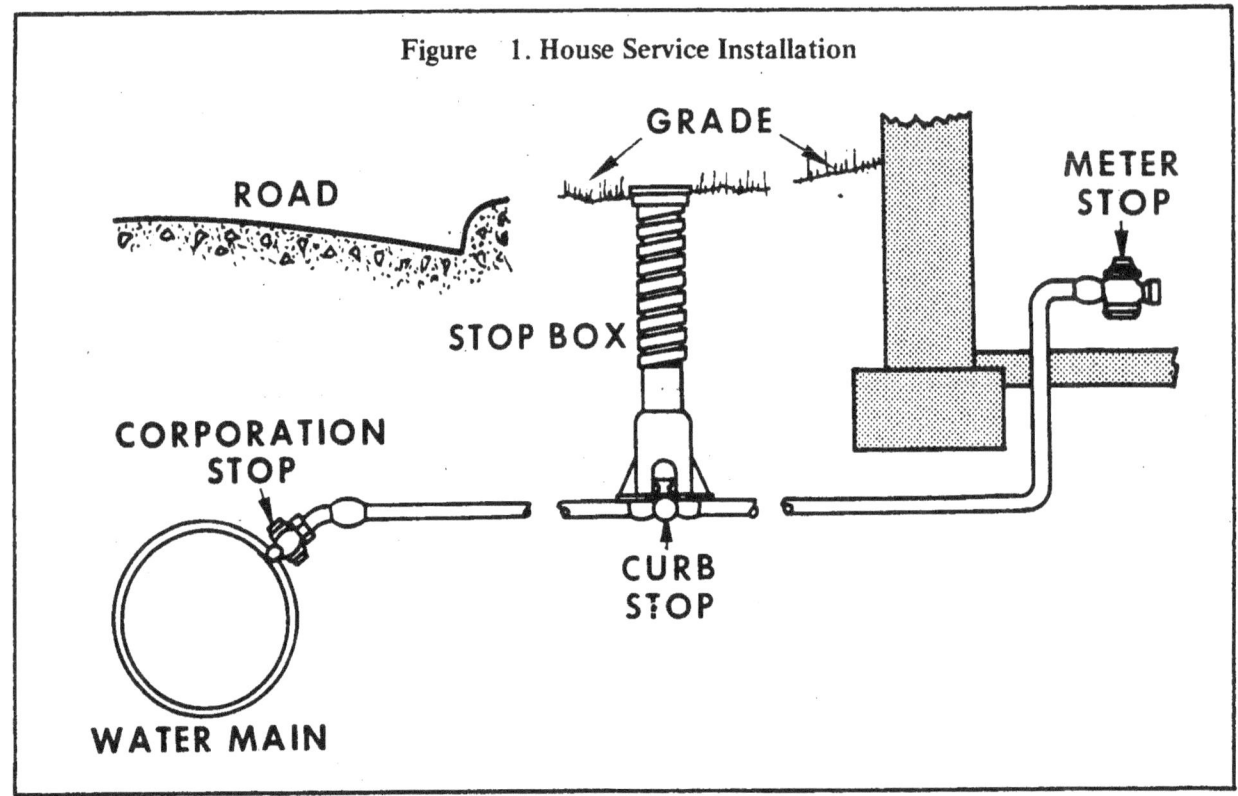

Figure 1. House Service Installation

- d **Meter stop** — The meter stop is a valve placed on the street side of the water meter to isolate the meter for installation or maintenance. Many codes require a gate valve on the house side of the meter to shut off water for house plumbing repairs. The curb and meter stops are not to be used frequently and can be ruined in a short time if used very frequently.

- e **Water meter** — The water meter is a device used to measure the amount of water used in the house. It is usually the property of the city and is a very delicate instrument that should not be abused.

  Since the electric system is usually grounded to the water line, a grounding loop-device should be installed around the meter. Many meters come with a yoke that maintains electrical continuity even though the meter is removed.

2. **Hot and Cold Water Main Lines:** The hot and cold water main lines are usually hung from the basement ceiling and are attached to the water meter and hot-water tank on one side and the fixture supply risers on the other.

These pipes should be installed in a neat manner and should be supported by pipe hangers or straps of sufficient strength and number to prevent sagging.

Hot and cold water lines should be approximately 6 inches apart unless the hot water line is insulated. This is to insure that the cold water line does not pick up heat from the hot water line.

The supply mains should have a drain valve or stop and waste valve in order to remove water from the system for repairs. These valves should be on the low end of the line or on the end of each fixture riser.

- a **The fixture risers** start at the basement main and rise vertically to the fixtures on the upper floors. In a one-family dwelling, riser branches will usually proceed from the main riser to each fixture grouping. In any event the fixture risers should not depend on the branch risers for support but should be supported with a pipe bracket.

Figure 2. Water Distribution System for Small Residence

b   Each fixture is then connected to the branch riser by a separate line. The last fixture on a line is usually connected directly to the branch riser. Figure 2 is a diagram of a typical single-family-residence water supply system.

3   Hot Water Heaters: Hot water heaters are usually powered by electricity, fuel oil, gas, or in rare cases, coal or wood. They consist of a space for heating the water and a storage tank for providing hot water over a limited period of time.

All hot water heaters should be fitted with a temperature-pressure relief valve no matter what fuel is used.

This valve will operate when either the temperature or the pressure becomes too high due to an interruption of the water supply or a faulty thermostat.

Figure 3 shows the correct installation of a hot water heater.

4   Pipe Sizes: The size of basement mains and risers depends on the number of fixtures supplied. However, a ¾ inch pipe is usually the minimum size used. This allows for deposits on the pipe due to hardness in the water and will usually give satisfactory volume and pressure.

B   Drainage System

The water supply brought into the house and used is discharged through the drainage system. This system is either a sanitary drainage system carrying just interior waste water or a combined system carrying interior waste and roof runoff. The sanitary system will be discussed first.

1   Sanitary Drainage System: The proper sizing of the sanitary drain or house drain depends on the number of fixtures it serves. The usual

Figure 3. Proper Water Heater Installation

minimum size is 6 inches in diameter. The materials used are usually cast iron, vitrified clay, plastic, and in rare cases, lead. For proper flow in the drain the pipe should be sized so that it flows approximately one-half full. This ensures proper scouring action so that the solids contained in the waste will not be deposited in the pipe.

a **Sizing of house drain** — The Uniform Plumbing Code Committee has developed a method of sizing of house drains in terms of "fixture units." One "fixture unit" equals approximately 7½ gallons of water per minute. This is the surge flow-rate of water discharged from a wash basin in 1 minute. All other fixtures have been related to this unit.

A table fixture unit values is shown in Table 1.

The maximum number of fixture units attached to a sanitary drain is shown in Table 2.

b **Grade of house drain** — A house drain or building sewer should be sloped toward the sewer to ensure scouring of the drain. Figure 4 shows the results of proper and improper pitch of a house drain.

The usual pitch of a house or building sewer is ¼ inch fall in 1 foot of length.

Table 1. FIXTURE UNIT VALUES

Fixture	Units
Lavatory/wash basin	1
Kitchen sink	2
Bathtub	2
Laundry tub	2
Combination fixture	3
Urinal	5
Shower bath	2
Floor drain	1
Slop sinks	3
Water closet	6
One bathroom group (water closet, lavatory, bathtub, and shower; or water closet, lavatory, and shower)	8
180 square feet of roof drained	1

c **House drain installation** — A typical house drain installation is shown in Figure 5. Typical branch connections to the main are shown in Figure 6.

d **Fixture and branch drains** — A branch drain is a waste pipe that collects the waste from two or more fixtures and conveys it to the building or house sewer. It is sized in the same way as the house sewer, taking into account that all water closets must have a minimum 3-inch diameter drain, and

Table 2. SANITARY DRAIN SIZES

	Maximum number of fixture units		
Diameter of pipe, in.	Slope 1/8"/Ft.	Slope 1/4"/Ft.	Slope 1/2"/Ft.
1¼	1	1	1
1½	2	2	3
2	5	6	8
3	15	18	21
4	84	96	114
6	300	450	600
8	990	1,392	2,220
12	3,084	4,320	6,912

*A water closet must enter a 3 inch diameter drain and no more than 2 water closets may enter a 3 inch horizontal branch.

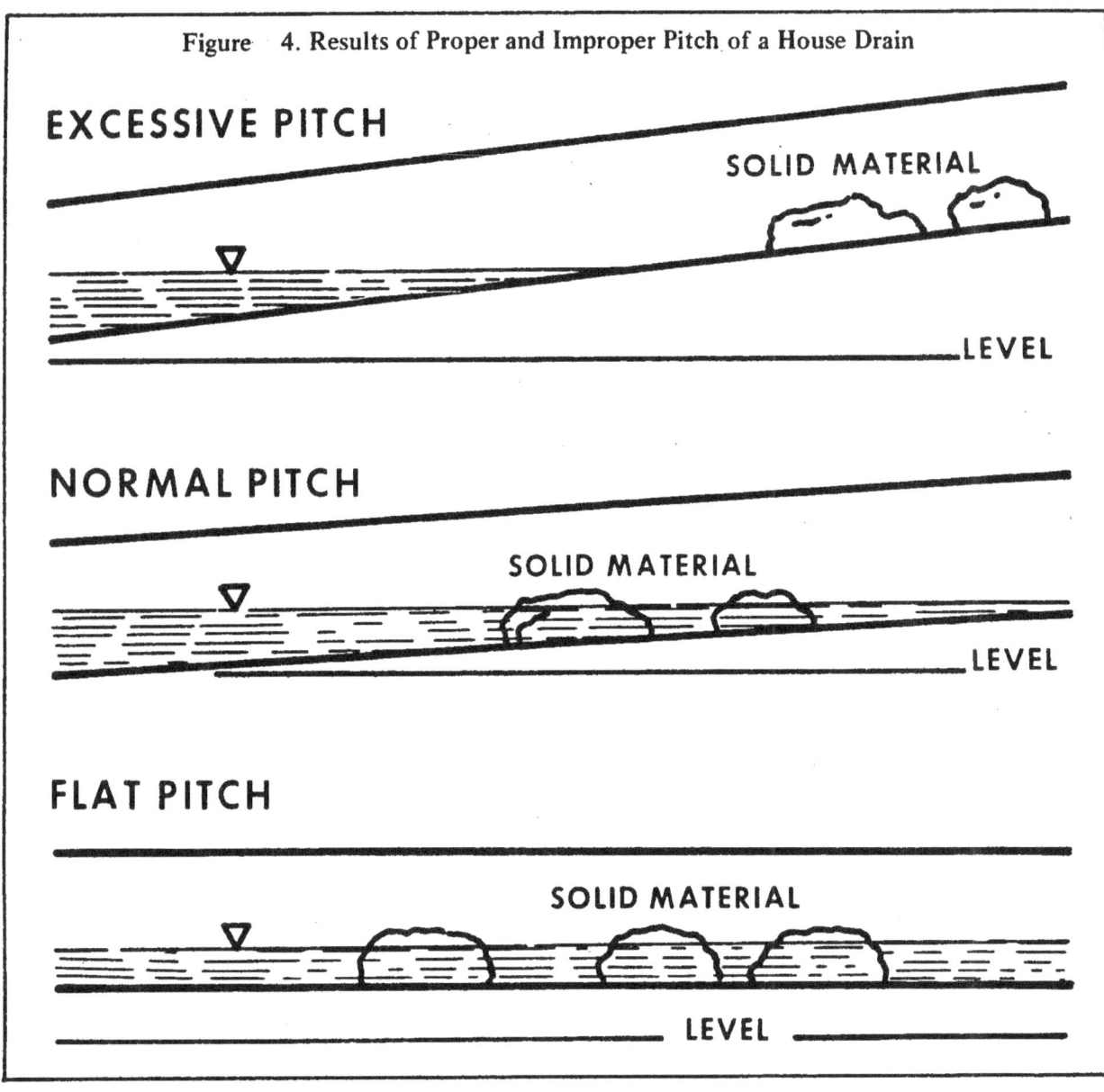

Figure 4. Results of Proper and Improper Pitch of a House Drain

only two water closets may connect into one 3-inch drain.

All branch drains must join the house drain with a "Y"-type fitting as shown in Figure 6. The same is true for fixture drains joining branch drains.

The "Y" fitting is used to eliminate, as much as possible, the deposit of solids in or near the connection. A build-up of these solids will cause a blockage in the drain.

The recommended minimum size of fixture drain is shown in Table 3.

e **Traps** — A plumbing trap is a device used in a waste system to prevent the passage of sewer gas into the structure and yet not hinder the fixture's discharge to any great extent. All fixtures connected to a household plumbing system should have a trap installed in the line.

Table 3. MINIMUM FIXTURE SERVICE

Fixture	Supply line, in.	Vent line, in.	Drain line, in.
Bathtub	½	1½	1½-2
Kitchen sink	½	1½	1½
Lavatory	3/8	1¼	1¼
Laundry sink	½	1½	1½
Shower	½	2	2
Water closet (tank)	3/8	3	3

Figure 5. Typical House Drain Installation

Figure 6. Typical Branch Connections to the Main

The effect of sewer gases on the human body are known; many are extremely harmful. Additionally, certain sewer gases are explosive. A trap will prevent these gases from passing into the structure.

1) "P" trap — The most common trap found today is the "P" trap. Figure 6-7 is a drawing of a "P" trap.

The depth of the seal in a trap is usually 2 inches. A deep seal trap has a 4-inch seal.

As was mentioned earlier, the purpose of a trap is to seal out sewer gases from the structure. Since a plumbing system is subject to wide variations in flow, and this flow originates in many different sections of the system, there is a wide variation in pressures in the waste lines. These pressure differences tend to destroy the water seal in the trap.

To counteract this problem mechanical traps were introduced. It has been found, however, that the corrosive liquids flowing in the system corrode or jam these mechanical traps. It is for this reason that most plumbing codes prohibit mechanical traps.

There are many manufacturers of traps, and all have varied the design somewhat. Figures 8 and 9 show various types of "P" traps. The "P" trap is usually found in lavatories, sinks, urinals, drinking fountains, showers, and other installations that do not discharge a great deal of water.

Figure 7. Diagram of a "P" Trap

Figure 8. Various Types of "P" Traps

2) Drum trap — The drum trap is another water seal-type trap. They are usually used in the 4- x 5-inch or 4- x 8-inch sizes. These traps have a greater sealing capacity than the "P" trap and pass large amounts of water quickly. Figure 10 shows a drum trap.

Drum traps are commonly connected to bathtubs, foot baths, sitz baths, and modified shower baths. Figure 11 shows a drum trap connected to a bathtub and shower.

Figure 9. Traps on Wall-hung Fixtures

Figure 10. A 4 x 8 Inch Drum Trap

Figure 11. (a) Drum Trap on Bathtub Outlet; (b) Drum Trap on Shower Installation

3) Objectionable traps — The "S" trap and the ¾ "S" trap should not be used in plumbing installations. They are almost impossible to ventilate properly, and the ¾ "S" trap forms a perfect siphon.

The bag trap, an extreme form of "S" trap, is seldom found. Figure 12 shows these types of "S" traps.

Figure 13 shows one type of mechanically sealed trap. Any trap that depends on a moving part for its effectiveness is usually inadequate and has been prohibited by the local plumbing codes.

Figure 12. Types of "S" Traps

FULL S-TRAP   ¾ S-TRAP   BAG TRAP

Figure 13. Mechanically Sealed Trap

Figure 14. Partition Traps

Figure 15. Examples of Direct Siphonage: (a) Seal Intact, (b) Fixture Discharging, (c) Loss of Seal

Figure 14 shows various types of internal partition traps. These traps work, but their design usually results in their being higher priced than the "P" or drum traps.

It should be remembered that traps are used only to prevent the escape of sewer gas into the structure. They do not compensate for pressure variations. Only proper venting will eliminate pressure problems.

f **Ventilation** — A plumbing system is ventilated to prevent trap seal loss, material deterioration, and flow retardation.

Figure 16. Loss of Trap Seal

Figure 17. Loss of Trap Seal as a Result of Back Pressure

1) Trap seal loss — The seal in a plumbing trap may be lost due to siphonage (direct and indirect or momentum), back pressure, evaporation, capillary attraction, or wind effect. The first two named are probably the most common causes of loss.

If a waste pipe is placed vertically after the fixture trap, as in an "S" trap, the waste water continues to flow after the fixture is emptied and clears the trap. This is caused by the pressure of air on the fixture water's being greater than the pressure of air in the waste pipe. The action of the water discharging into the waste pipe removes the air from that pipe and thereby causes a negative pressure in the waste line.

In the case of indirect or momentum siphonage, the flow of water past the entrance to a fixture drain in the waste pipe removes air from the fixture drain. This reduces the air pressure in the fixture drain, and the entire assembly acts as an aspirator such as the physician uses to spray an infected throat. Figures 15 and 16 show examples of siphonage.

2) Back pressure — The flow of water in a soil pipe varies according to the fixtures being used. A lavatory gives a small flow and a water closet a large flow. Small flows tend to cling to the sides of the pipe, but large ones form a slug of waste as they drop. As this slug of water falls down the pipe the air in front of it becomes pressurized. As the pressure builds it seeks an escape point. This point is either a vent or a fixture outlet. If the vent is plugged or there is no vent, the only escape for this air is the fixture outlet. The air pressure forces the trap seal up the pipe into the fixture. If the pressure is great enough the seal is blown out of the fixture entirely. Figures 17 and 18 illustrate this type of problem.

3) Vent sizing — Vent pipe installation is similar to that of soil and waste pipe. The same fixture unit criteria are used. Table 3 shows minimum vent pipe sizes.

Vent pipes of less than 1¼ inches in diameter should not be used. Vents smaller than this diameter tend to clog and do not perform their function.

4) Individual fixture ventilation — Figure 19 shows a typical installation of a wall-hung plumbing unit. This type of ventilation is generally used for sinks, lavatories, drinking fountains, and so forth.

Figure 20 shows a typical installation of a bathtub or shower ventilation system.

Figure 19. Individual Ventilation of Lavatories, Sinks, Drinking Fountains, etc.

Figure 20. Individual Ventilation of Bathtubs, Showers and Urinals

Figure 18. Loss of Trap Seal By Capillary Attraction

Figure 21 shows the proper vent connection for a water closet or slop sink. The water closet can be either a tank type or a flushometer valve type.

5) Unit venting — Figures 22 to 24 picture a back-to-back ventilation system for various common plumbing fixtures. The unit venting system is commonly used in apartment buildings. This type of system saves a great deal of money and space when fixtures are placed back to back in separate apartments.

Figure 21. Individual Ventilation of Water Closets, Clinic Sinks, or Slop Sinks

Figure 22. Unit Vent Method of Ventilating Wall-hung Fixture Traps

Figure 23. Unit Vent used in Bathtub Installation

Figure 24. Unit Vent used in Water Closet Installation

Figure 25 shows a double combination "Y" used for joining the fixtures to the common soil pipe. The deflectors are to prevent waste from one fixture flowing back up into the waste in the attached fixture on the other side of the wall.

6) Wet venting — Wet venting of a plumbing system is common in household bathroom fixture grouping. It is exactly what the name implies: the vent pipe is used as a waste line. Figure 26 shows a typical wet-vent installation in a home.

7) Total drainage system — Up to now we have talked about the drain, soil waste, and vent systems of a plumbing system separately. For a working system, however, they must all be connected. Figures 27 through 32 show some typical drainage systems that are found in homes and small apartment buildings.

Figure 25. Double Combination Y and 1/8 Bend with Deflectors

Figure 26. West Vent Used in Connection With Bathroom Group of Fixtures

Figure 27. Drain Soil Waste and Vent Pipe Layout

Figure 28. Plumbing Layout for a Two-Story Residence, Showing Individual Ventilation of Fixtures

Figure 29. Typical Plumbing Layout for a Two-story Apartment Building

Figure 30. Plumbing Layout for a Duplex Residence

Figure 31. Direct Cross Connection

Figure 32. Cross Connection

www.ingramcontent.com/pod-product-compliance
Lightning Source LLC
Chambersburg PA
CBHW081814300426
44116CB00014B/2351